"This new book helps to fill a huge gap in the world of Christian spiritual writing: the home. Tim and Sue Muldoon's lovely work is a warm, practical, inviting, user-friendly, and family-tested manual on ways to find God in the complex world of the family. Too often books on family life are written either by celibates with no lived experience of changing diapers, or by fathers or mothers who give the impression that their family is the exemplar of all that is good. *Six Sacred Rules for Families* wisely grounds itself in the Gospels, but also reflects the authors' real-life experience in struggling to find God in the messy and often beautiful place where we all begin our spiritual journeys: in the family."

James Martin, S.J.
Author of *The Jesuit Guide to (Almost) Everything*

"Tim and Sue Muldoon have done something wonderful, here: they've managed to impart and apply Ignatian wisdom to the realities of family life, and in the process they've communicated a spiritual perspective that is immensely valuable to the stressful job of parenting. I loved this book and couldn't put it down. Although my children are grown, the insights and tools shared here are as applicable to the parenting of adult children as to young ones, because they are rooted in true wisdom and can only strengthen the family dynamic. I just wish these rules had been in my hands twenty years ago!"

Elizabeth Scalia
Author of *Strange Gods*

"Tim and Sue Muldoon have created something rare indeed: a quick and enjoyable read worth ten times its weight in gold. You will want to enjoy it over and over, highlighting and underlining as you go. This delightful resource is overflowing with practical wisdom for every parent who longs to give their children the treasures of a living faith in Jesus Christ. Endearing and entertaining personal stories from the Muldoons' marriage and family life illuminate simple but powerful spiritual lessons—lessons accessible enough to embolden even the most timid among us to draw nearer to Jesus Christ, and to bring our children into vibrant relationship with Him."

Lisa Mladinich
Author of *Be an Amazing Catechist*

"Tim and Sue Muldoon have beautifully captured practical ways of being a life-giving domestic church. With real-life examples and illustrations they drive home the vital message of keeping Christ at the center of family life. I highly recommend this book to parents and grandparents as well as pastors and educators."

Bonnie Mack
Marriage and Family Minister
Archdiocese of Cincinnati

"Deeply schooled in scripture and classic—especially Ignatian—spirituality, Tim and Sue Muldoon offer their readers inspirational and practical stories about their own search for the sacred ground beneath the often shifting landscape of family life. *Six Sacred Rules for Families* is a thoughtful and welcome reflection on what it means for both parents and their children to embark on the ultimate adventure of finding God in all things."

Wendy M. Wright
Professor of Theology
Creighton University

"Young parents will find in this gem of a book an invitation to see God's presence in the struggles and joys of creating and sustaining a family. Tim and Sue Muldoon reflect on their experiences of cultivating spiritual practices in their home and offer concrete advice for keeping love at the center of family life. A great resource both for those who struggle with faith and for strong believers who want to live their faith more deeply."

Julie Hanlon Rubio
Associate Professor of Christian Ethics
St. Louis University

TIM & SUE MULDOON

SIXSACRED

RULES_{FOR}FAMILIES

A Spirituality for the Home

ave maria press AMP notre dame, indiana

Founded in 1865, Ave Maria Press is a ministry of the United States Province of Holy Cross.

www.avemariapress.com

Paperback: ISBN-10 1-59471-372-3, ISBN-13 978-1-59471-372-9

E-book: ISBN-10 1-59471-373-1, ISBN-13 978-1-59471-373-6

Cover images © Thinkstock.com.

Cover and text design by Brian C. Conley.

Printed and bound in the United States of America.

Library of Congress Cataloging-in-Publication Data

Muldoon, Tim.
  Six sacred rules for families : a spirituality for the home / Tim and Sue Muldoon.
     pages cm
  Includes bibliographical references.
  ISBN 978-1-59471-372-9 (pbk.) -- ISBN 1-59471-372-3 (pbk.)
  1. Families--Religious life. 2. Spiritual life--Christianity. I. Title.
  BV4526.3.M85 2013
  248.4--dc23

                              2013022191

CONTENTS

INTRODUCTION

Are you intrigued by the idea that there can be, as this book's sub-title suggests, a spirituality for the home? Perhaps you tend to connect the word "spirituality" with what you seek when you leave your home life behind: feelings of peace, a sense of connection with the world, an awareness of the holy—you know, the kinds of things that elude you when you're in the midst of making dinner, paying bills, or cleaning up after your children. What this book proposes is a view of spirituality as very much grounded in everyday life. And what lies under this proposal is an even more radical suggestion, namely that everyday life (on the one hand) and those feelings of peace, connection with the world, and awareness of the holy (on the other) are meant to go together. To say it a little more forcefully, we are suggesting that authentic spirituality is not something above or beyond everyday life but embedded right in the messy midst of it.

To illustrate this point, we will be exploring the implications of the way that Jesus invited his listeners to look for what he called the "Kingdom of God" or "Kingdom of Heaven" unfolding right under their noses. What is most significant about his many allusions to the Kingdom is the fact that his descriptions focus on the "here-and-nowness" of it, in contrast to a mistaken idea that it's an add-on to ordinary human life to be anticipated after we die. Don't look for it in any other place but where you are living right in this very moment, he seems to be saying to his followers. As parents, we often find ourselves asking the question, "What might that mean for us?"

We've condensed our answers over the years into six rules that can be described as basic statements of how to look at the world the way Jesus did. The inspiration for these rules is a little book penned by Saint Ignatius of Loyola in the sixteenth century called *The Spiritual Exercises*. His manual for cultivating Christian prayer has influenced millions of people who have encountered it in retreat houses and schools all over the world. Quite simply, Ignatius wanted to invite people to consider Jesus' way of looking at things not primarily as a set of doctrines established centuries ago. While doctrines continue to be important to the life of the Church, they are not usually what draw people into imitating Jesus. Instead, Ignatius wanted people to have an experience of knowing God the way Jesus did—to fall in love with God—so that everything else in their lives made sense in light of that love. Once you fall in love, everything changes.

We've discovered in our prayer and in our lives as parents that it's possible to apply this same insight specifically to family life, and so we offer the rules as easy-to-remember takeaways. Why rules? Quite simply, because rules allow everyone to enjoy a game. The same is true of a professional football game, a business transaction, and family life. Rules keep everyone on the same page; rules help us plan for the future and enjoy the present.

Early in the Church's history, figures such as Saint Benedict developed rules to guide communal life so that everyone might help one another achieve lasting joy in their lives before God. Religious men and women today still use Benedict's Rule because it has profoundly shaped people's ability to lead a holy life for some fifteen centuries. We are suggesting that our "Rules for Family Spirituality" similarly aim at helping families orient their shared life toward the common good of living in love. Like a monastery, a family is a group of people who live together and share the ups and downs of daily life. Food preparation, sleeping arrangements, recreational time, cleaning up, and helping one another grow are common to both kinds of communities. Further, both kinds of communities are rooted in the way God has created people to enter into relationships rooted in love. The rules we are proposing are intended to help parents name what they hope for in their family life so that the members of the family—the "domestic church"—might help one another grow in love.

Now, full disclosure: our family doesn't perfectly reflect these rules every day—we doubt that anyone's family does or even can. We are not perfectly pious people, living blissfully conflict-free lives according to a preordained divine plan. Any parent understands that raising children is about living within the tension of knowing what is good for them (and ourselves) while at the same time negotiating the basic reality of what is happening right now. Sure, we know our children need balanced meals, but sometimes the chicken nuggets or hot dogs are all we can get them to eat. We know they must learn to behave well toward one another, but some days all we can do is separate them and keep them from hurting one another. Still, the rules (whether for nutrition, good psychological health, or—in this case—a strong faith life) help give us a compass point, both when the skies are clear and when there are storms.

RULES FOR FAMILY SPIRITUALITY

1. God brings our family together on pilgrimage.
2. Our love for one another leads to joy.
3. Our family doesn't care about "success."
4. God stretches our family toward his Kingdom.
5. God will help us.
6. We must learn which desires lead us to freedom.

In the following chapters, we'll explore what these rules might mean for living our family lives more authentically, more freely, more lovingly, and more joyfully. Throughout these pages, you'll see numerous callouts that emphasize a point or raise a question for consideration. These might be good topics for you and someone you love to discuss in your reflection on your own parenting. And at the end of the book are a lot of practical suggestions that you might want to consider applying to your family life. So whether you take this book slowly, reading it page by page, or whether you focus on these callouts as catalysts for conversation, our hope is that you may come to see your family life as the place where the Holy Spirit, in the words of Gerard Manley Hopkins, "broods with warm breast and with ah! bright wings!"

PART ONE

A NEW VISION OF FAMILY LIFE

CHAPTER ONE

CHANGE YOUR PERSPECTIVE

If you've picked up this book on family spirituality or if someone in your life has passed this book along, you've likely come to the realization that family life summons from us a real need for God. Chances are you are caught up in the busyness that all the people around you are immersed in as well; you sometimes feel stressed and pulled in different directions; you have hopes and desires, fears and anxieties for yourself and the people you love. You may or may not be religious in the sense of going to church very often, but you have a hunger for meaning, beauty, and hope. You feel yourself reaching out, however uncertainly, for a God who can somehow bring to harmony all these churning, relentless feelings.

What you are likely experiencing in this hunger is an already-real desire for God, however unclear it may seem from day to day. In the Christian tradition, that hunger has a name: faith. Far from a kind of certainty about everything, faith is, at its most basic level, a way of living with hopeful conviction that life is meaningful. Parenting, we have found, necessitates that kind of conviction. Have you ever considered how much you are already living a life of faith?

Think about it: you are always making decisions about things you can have no certainty about. You've pledged to live your life with other people who have the same desire for freedom that you do. All of you have your individual hopes and dreams, and all of you have ideas about what you want to do from day to day, but somehow you manage to press on together. Of course, there are periods when living together is hard, and those times can make us question whether we know what we're doing as parents. But the very desire to press on is itself a symptom of the life of faith.

> **Parenting is sometimes like driving in the dark.**

The biblical author of the Letter to the Hebrews put it this way: "Faith is the realization of what is hoped for and evidence of things not seen" (11:1). Starting and living family life is almost never according to plan. The image that comes to mind is driving in the dark: you can only see as far as your headlights allow, but still that's enough to drive across the country.

If you're like us, there have been times in your family life when you happen upon an unexpected joy, an unexpected sense of rightness in the world—a sense of "realization of what is hoped for," even though you may not have had the words to name that hope. Similarly, if you're like us, you have also had days when you had to trudge ahead because work was hard, the school schedule was relentless, you had little time for showing love to your spouse or reaching out to your friends, and you wondered whether your decision to enter into family life was a good one. You felt, on some level, the need for "evidence of things not seen"—that is, a sense that in the end, the daily labor of living as a family culminates in something beautiful.

A MATTER OF FAITH

"Faith is the realization of what is hoped for and evidence of things not seen" (Heb 11:1).

- Do you find it easy to act in faith?
- Do you see your family life as dependent upon faith?
- Do you connect the life of your family with an explicit faith in God?

We often wrestle with questions of how our family can live in faith. Much of what we learned *about* faith came from our parents. Both of us went to Mass and Sunday school as kids; we learned prayers; we celebrated the sacraments. But as we got older—and especially when we went off to college—we began to think of faith less as something to *learn* and more as something to *rely on* in the face of life decisions. Taking faith seriously enough to rely on led to tough questions. We had to ask ourselves if we were willing to shape our entire lives around a faith we had learned as children but were now beginning to own. Were we willing to grow in faith, even at the risk of going to places without a clear map—places that people who did not live a life of faith might think irrelevant or illogical? Would we go deep into our faith, knowing that God would somehow guide our life choices? Would we be willing to share with our children what we learned?

There's an old song that captures what's at stake regarding to family life choices. Harry Chapin's 1974 song "Cat's in the Cradle" tells the story of a man who is too busy to spend time with his young son. The adoring son vows that he is "gonna be like you, Dad." His words are proven true but not in the way the father expected. The adult son becomes just as busy as his father had been when he was a boy, leading the father to a somber reflection: "And as I hung up the phone it occurred to me / He'd grown up just like me." It's a sad song perhaps in part because it expresses a reality with which many can identify: the unrequited yearning for time alone with a parent. Let's face it—parenting takes massive amounts of time and energy to just keep a household running, from working to paying bills to shopping to cleaning to helping with homework, and so on. Carving out special time with children can be difficult, particularly in times of financial stress. Aren't there any rules to ensure our choices will actually lead us to what will make us happy?

ASSESSING FAMILY PRIORITIES

Spend time in prayer considering what you value as a parent.
- What will you remember on your deathbed?
- What will you hope you have passed on to your children?
- How do you hope they will remember you?
- Consider keeping a journal to remain mindful of what is most important and what is fleeting.

> God is in charge;
> our lives have meaning;
> and love is a window
> to eternity.

Take another example, this time from the 1989 film *Dead Poets Society*. Set at an elite prep school, it focuses on the tension between parental expectation and youthful idealism. A student named Leonard, through the influence of an exceptional teacher, discovers a love for poetry and drama. Leonard desperately wants to perform in a play, but because of his father's disapproval, he keeps his participation secret. His performance in a Shakespearean play is a triumph, but it leaves his father furious. Threatened with being pulled out of school, Leonard despairs of his future and kills himself.

By most popular measures, Leonard and his family are winners, with wealth and prestige and a bright future. But what

Change your perspective. The Kingdom of God is right in front of you.

makes Leonard's life so tragic is the feeling of being trapped. It is an unsettling film in the sense that it raises the question of what to live for. If wealth and a career track through the best schools into a high-powered medical career can drive a young person to suicide, then what else is worth striving for?

These two stories point to a challenge that often goes unnamed in a family's life: how to answer the question, "What exactly are we living for?" Most of the time, we operate on autopilot, more or less following the patterns we learned as children in our families of origin. We work; we divide up chores; we send the kids to school; we take family vacations; we celebrate holidays, and so on. The big moments may remind us there's a big picture, but still it's easy to get caught up in the day-to-day work of life.

The idea of family is very much an idea rooted in faith—it is always about looking toward the good of the ones we love in the face of an uncertain future. It is about vulnerability, risk and a willingness to love amidst pain and sometimes crushing disappointment. But to say that family is rooted in faith is not to say that it's completely blind or that it's completely about luck or fate or the unknown. For followers of Jesus, it's about faith that God is in charge, that our lives have meaning, that love is a window to eternity. In the light of Jesus' faith, family is ultimately about a life's purpose. To say it a little differently, nothing of family life is meaningless: God can orchestrate joys and griefs, successes and failures, expressions of love or experiences of pain toward something beautiful. To persuade his followers of this truth, Jesus' preaching returned again and again to the theme of the Kingdom unfolding right in our midst, under our noses: "change your hearts, for the kingdom of heaven is at hand" (Mt 3:2, 10:7; Mk 1:15).[1] Family faith is ultimately about seeing our lives not through the limited perspectives of our own desires but rather coming to see them through "Kingdom eyes," the way Jesus described.

What are Kingdom eyes? They are a way of looking at the world not as a series of disconnected events—some bad, some good—but as an ongoing project in which God is trying to entice people to cooperate with him in freedom to build a world governed by love. We have found that most parents, even if they are not explicitly religious, believe this on some level. They want their children to grow up in a world of love rather than of cutthroat competition and violence.

Think about it for a moment: What persuades you that love is worth practicing? What makes you think that raising a child is worth all the sacrifice and life change it demands? If you love, you already look at the world through Kingdom eyes, however unclear. Perhaps what Jesus wants most is to help you clarify your vision.

What we are proposing is really very simple: a change in perspective. That change is about using Kingdom eyes in a very specific way: to see that everything we do in the course of every day is in cooperation with a God who loves us and who is constantly inviting us to be love in the world, first toward our families and then toward everyone else. That kind of perspective emerges through the regular practice of prayer.

Prayer is the language of friendship with God.[2] And like any good friendship, it will have its moments of joy and heartache, of stress and tenderness, of gratefulness and anger. Sometimes the friendship will be tested by life changes: suffering and death, work stress, difficulties in relationships. Other times it will swell with the joy of discovery: a new child, a new home, success at work. The good of friendship, Aristotle once observed, is that it is a good in itself as well as a good that moves friends in a common direction. Friendship with God means making an effort to continue the conversation, both in good times and in bad, for the sake of both the friendship itself and the goods that emerge from the common direction we walk with God. We are suggesting that cultivating this friendship at all times will yield goods both for parents and for the children who imitate them.

Do not think of prayer as a chore—as a hard lesson gained by years of study in a remote mountaintop monastery. Rather, imagine your prayer as simply your daily conversation with God, your chance to catch up with the most intimate friend in your life. Greet God when you wake up; talk with God as you shower; chatter with God as you help your children get dressed or get them ready for school; dream with God as you prepare meals; lean on God as you comfort your child who has gotten sick. And teach your children to pray by imitating the ways you pray.

In our experience, learning prayer and coming to see God as a friend was not always easy. Before we explain the rules, we'll first tell you a little about how they came to emerge as clear guidelines for us in our own family life.

CHAPTER TWO

OUR DESIRES, GOD'S DESIRES

Long before we met, some formative experiences shaped the way we came to understand our hopes for family life and the way we would bring faith to bear on that kind of life. When Sue was younger, she dreamed about having a family. Growing up, she was the oldest of four children in a very tight Irish-Catholic family, and from an early age, she saw life through the lens of responsibility to parents and younger siblings. Early on, she developed a sensitivity toward the common good that made her perhaps less individualistic than some of her peers. She was often the babysitter; the one who comforted her mom when her dad had to travel for work; the one who set a good example. There were times when all this responsibility was difficult, but for the most part, family-mindedness gave her a sense of place in the world. As she grew older, she began to nurture the hope that she would meet the right man and start her own family. Even in high school and college, when having a decent social life usually takes priority over thinking about the future, there was in the back of her mind the lingering question, "Can I see this guy as the father of my children?"

When Tim first met Sue, he had no intention of getting married or starting a family—he intended to be a lifelong bachelor. He was a couple years younger than Sue, and his hopes and dreams for the future focused more on professional goals than on marriage and family. He's the second of four children. When he was in junior high school, his sister was born. Three years later, his brother was born. Tim had lots of experience helping his parents when his siblings were babies; he learned about changing diapers, feeding, playing with them in their toddler years, and helping them when they got to school age. Perhaps all this early experience of being a kind of third parent made fatherhood seem like just a lot of work.

> I know the plans
> I have for you,
> says the Lord:
> plans to give you
> a future full of hope.
>
> JEREMIAH 29:11

Tim's attitude toward marriage began to change after meeting Sue, getting to know her, and growing in the conviction that he wanted to spend his life with her. Over time, he began to see the world through her eyes and to ask himself whether what she wanted out of life was also what he wanted. For him, the decision to let go of his more self-centered desires in order to discern the desires that they shared was the paradigmatic act of faith. "Faith is the realization of what is hoped for and evidence of things not seen." That was exactly how it felt: forming a relationship with her and letting go of his earlier desires was the realization of a hope nestled in his heart that had as yet gone unnamed.

There's a movie called *Sliding Doors* that tells the story of possible futures changed by a decision regarding whether or not to board a train. That one decision creates alternate universes. A major theme in the film has to do with the relationship between freedom and fate and the question of how specific choices we make affect lifelong change. As we look back on our early relationship, it's easy to ask that kind of question of ourselves. Had we not taken the risk of telling each other what we were hoping for, our lives would likely have gone in different directions. Tim would have continued his studies, while Sue would have gone to live in another part of the country to continue hers, and our lives might never have crossed paths again. Instead, we acted in faith—faith that our willingness to forge a relationship over long distance would bring us joy.

Our early life together was saturated in acts of faith in each other. We had little money; we had school and work to negotiate, requiring us to discern where to live and how to support each other. What made it possible was a growing and deepening sense of trust in each other. But there was also our shared Catholic faith, our shared trust that God had given us hearts for the family life we felt ourselves called to.

The first real test of our faith came when, early in our marriage, we faced what seemed a catastrophic loss: the inability to conceive a child. Suddenly, the question of faith was not just a vague theory or a habit of churchgoing. It was a confrontation with a situation we found intensely difficult, throwing us into confusion about who we believed God was—and whether we wanted to be friends with him. What sustained us was the constant communication about what we were thinking and feeling and going through. We still went to church out of habit, but there were times when it was particularly difficult. We remember one Mother's Day Mass when Sue had to leave in tears during the blessing of the mothers in the congregation. God seemed so distant, so inaccessible. Why would he not grant Sue her heart's desire, one she had come to believe was good and holy? Why would God test her faith this way?

We found this time in our lives incredibly hard. Tim had to watch the person he loved go through suffering that touched almost every aspect of our shared life, from medical tests to decisions about money to talk about what our future was going to look like. Anyone who has struggled with infertility knows how consuming it can be, rendering even our sex life a repeated clinical failure. Getting to the beginning of family life was a struggle we had not fully prepared ourselves for. How could we have?

This struggle lasted for years and took us through every kind of psychological stress. The only thing that sustained us was a shared faith in each other and, ultimately, in a God who could yet surprise us with the emergence of a new and different kind of hope. "Faith is the realization of what is hoped for and evidence of things not seen." What we found through the slow death of our hopes for biological children was a slow birth of hope for children through adoption.

SUSTAINING FAITH THROUGH DIFFICULTIES

- Have you had life experiences that have tested or even strangled your faith?
- How do you experience a desire for faith?
- Do you hope your children might learn from your experiences of faith?

That experience of slowly—and sometimes painfully—letting go of one desire in order to embrace a newer, more lasting one has emerged as a pattern for the work of God's grace in our lives. Through our shared faith, both in each other and in God, we have come to discover the many ways this pattern has impacted our family life over the years. Our life story is about faith and about how to cultivate our response to grace between ourselves and with our children.

There have been moments in our lives when the work of grace has been so transparent that they give meaning to all the work and struggle of daily life. As difficult as it was to let go of our hopes of conceiving children, the wide space carved out in our hearts by that experience allowed the inrushing of the Holy Spirit. In that holy space, we discovered a desire to adopt, from the unlikeliest of places, halfway across the world. "I know the plans I have for you, says the Lord: plans to give you a future full of hope" (Jer 29:11).

Sue proposed the idea of adopting early in our struggles with infertility. Initially, Tim pushed back against adopting, thinking it was a capitulation to a medical issue that needed to be addressed with smart thinking and good decision making. Over time, however, he began to listen to the voice of a different desire—one that Sue voiced to him and one that he eventually discovered sounding in his own heart. We wanted to be parents; adoption would allow our desire for children to meet the desire of a child for parents. Pain yielded to sadness, which yielded to openness, which yielded to hope, which yielded to joy when we ultimately chose to adopt. Faith was the realization of what we had hoped for.

Not long ago, we returned with our two daughters, Katie and Grace, to the place where we discovered God's grace in adoption. It was the summer of 2011, and the July sun was blazing, raising waves of heat off the pavement on a tree-lined street in the middle of Hefei, the capital city of Anhui Province, China. The four of us had set off by foot from our hotel just a block back, but already a quarter of the way to our destination, we were soaked in sweat. Katie, the eight-year-old, and Grace, eleven, were troopers, even though they did not really have a strong desire to come along. They weren't entirely sure they understood why we were walking from our hotel to another hotel, especially one that didn't even have a swimming pool.

After several ponderous minutes of walking, we parents marveled as we walked up the hill toward the front entrance. "We're here, girls—the Anhui Hotel!" we said, laughing, looking at each other, and marveling that the place had changed little in the past decade. "This is where it all started."

We were talking about the day when, just about ten years earlier, we met Grace for the first time. At the time, she was a sobbing and panicked ten-month-old, stressed to the core, understanding on some very deep level that something scary was happening. Her small, soft head had been hot and damp to the touch, and she was uttering a constant, repeated wail: "hummmmm-uhh . . . hummmmm-uhh." It had taken us quite a while just to calm her and give her some food before she abruptly fell asleep, exhausted, for the night.

Walking into that lobby had the effect of collapsing a decade of experiences into an intense moment of recollection. Same front desk; same stairway; same balcony, where we had stood with a video camera rolling as the bus from the orphanage had pulled up that December day. The main difference was the weather: Then it had been cold and gray, making the entire strange city feel dreary. This day in July, by contrast, was brilliant. This second trip to the city made us feel almost at home.

Ten years earlier, we knew we were embarking upon a life path that was, to say the least, unusual. Even then we knew that our first trip to China would not be our last: committing to the adoption of a Chinese orphan meant for us a commitment to a land and a people whom we would learn to embrace as family. Before long, we started the process to adopt Katie, and we made our second trip to China in September 2003. By then it was clear that a heritage trip would be in our future, but with the cost of travel, we understood it would have to wait some years.

Eight years later, here we were. The Anhui Hotel was the first stop on a tour of memories from our two previous trips. We would later visit both Grace's and Katie's orphanages as well as some of the places we'd seen during those first visits. We toured historic sites with the girls; ate great food; and met some wonderful people, including foster parents and former caregivers. We gained new friends. We received as gifts some early pictures of one of our girls. We built memories together as a family. We ended the trip with hearts full and bodies exhausted from travel.

Not long after that, we realized the trip had also unearthed a lingering desire to adopt again, and so we returned the following winter to meet our son, John. Here again we discovered God was whispering to us to open our hearts and our home to an orphan, even amidst a busy period of life when we had not previously imagined such a change. We discovered that God's desire for us can be richer than the desires that emerge in our daily lives.

When we were younger, the thought of building life plans around travel to China would have seemed exotic and strange. Today, though, it seems as natural as can be. The moments of profound meaning in our lives—the things that motivate our life choices, the things we work for, the things that occupy our thoughts when we are not driven from one immediate need to another—are what touch us most deeply and suggest to us that the contours of our experience are perhaps not as clearly defined as we often assume. But at the edges of those contours is the gentle yet powerful voice of God, who, in our experience, has invited us to take risks of love in the great hope of building lives of profound meaning. Big life changes—like falling in love, getting married, and birthing or adopting—can quickly call to mind our dependence on God. So too can moments of pain and suffering—illness or injury, divorce, and deaths of loved ones—reminding us that the world we inhabit is not one we can fully control. And so we have come to learn that at the calm center of the storm that is our daily life is a deep place where God calls to us in prayer. We continue to learn that truth, and we continue to hope we can share it with our children. And the rules, we've learned, help keep all of us moving together toward God.

CHAPTER THREE

AWARENESS IN EVERYDAY LIFE

It can be difficult for us to discover the work of grace in our everyday lives. The moments of profoundest meaning and emotional high make it seem like God is immediately present and anything is possible, but those moments must yield to the slow, repetitious pace of everyday life. And in times of difficulty, grace can seem altogether distant. Sustaining a life of faith, and sharing faith with our children, requires an approach beyond what we feel at any given moment.

The first step is to realize how much family life already calls forth from us a life of faith. Our daily life is circumscribed by the realities of sharing with others: what and when we eat, how we sleep, where and how we spend our time—all these things are influenced by the people in our home. Living with other people requires faith in their good will and faith that the hundred small sacrifices we make can lead to something beautiful together.

If you are a parent—especially of small children—you know these realities are often hilarious. They certainly stretch your imagination and maybe even your tolerance. In our home over the past week, a more or less average one, much of our energy was dedicated to curious things like bathroom use, the irritation caused by whining, the ways our bodies need nutrients, the problem with shoes cluttering the floor, the benefits of laundry hampers, the conjugation of Spanish verbs, the recipe for guacamole, and the schedule for basketball games.

And what is remarkable is that God is present in each one of these curious things, and we have to constantly remind ourselves of that truth. For us, discerning God's presence is sometimes as easy as opening our eyes. Other times, though, particularly when things get stressful, God can seem as distant as a good rest.

The Jesuit writer Anthony de Mello once shared an image that captures for us the challenge and opportunity of discerning ordinary family life as the place where God lives and breathes. A small fish went swimming, hoping to see for himself where the ocean was. A wise older fish told him, "You're swimming in it." The small fish, dissatisfied, observed that sure, there was water all around him, but that wasn't what he was after. "I'm looking for the OCEAN!" he said.

Too often, busy people are looking for God so much that they don't see God. Too often as parents, we are looking for some deep meaning, something that maybe reminds us of monks chanting, of beatific-faced religious sisters serving a dying person, or of a preacher expounding upon a deep theological truth—so much that we miss the incredibly obvious truth right under our noses. Family life is a life of faith, and as an act of faith, it is the place where we can learn love, and as the place where we can learn love, we can discern God.

When we first made the decision to adopt, our world changed. We realized how little we knew about adoption or even about parenting. We had to throw ourselves into the work of educating ourselves: meeting with the social worker, developing contacts with other adoptive parents, reading books and magazines about adoption and about China. We began learning a little Chinese, reading stories about the joys and challenges of families formed by adoption, and imagining what would lie ahead of us by taking the plunge to build our family this way.

An interesting thing happened. Somewhere along the process, we began to see adoption everywhere—in the news, in conversations with friends who had an adopted sister or cousin or parent, in movies, and on TV. Somehow just opening our eyes to adoption made it come alive and pervade our daily life, long before we even adopted a child of our own. We had developed an awareness of adoption, and as a result, we began to see it everywhere. Sue even developed a new kind of "radar" as we called it; she could just sense when we were near families with Chinese adoptees. More than once she approached total strangers and talked with them about the experience.

Awareness applies to the spiritual life as well. There is an old form of Ignatian prayer known as the Examen (see page 20) which is a kind of practice of reflection on one's past experiences, looking for places where one has felt God's presence. This prayer of awareness allows us the time to pause and recognize God even in the midst of difficult life situations. Over time, the practice of this prayer has helped us to notice how God moves in our lives in small, often quiet ways, beneath the loud

> You shall seek the Lord, your God; and you shall indeed find him when you search after him with your whole heart and your whole soul.
>
> DEUTERONOMY 4:29

clanging of the things that take our attention. We discover what is the starting point for a spiritual life: the deep sense that our experiences really *mean* something and that in reaching out toward the source and goal of that meaning, we encounter God.

THE EXAMEN PRAYER

1. Find a comfortable place where you can secure ten or fifteen quiet minutes. Have a journal handy.
2. Close your eyes and relax your body. Try deep breathing, stretching, or whatever else helps you eliminate distraction.
3. Invite the Holy Spirit to be with you in prayer, to help you learn to pray.
4. Offer God thanks for the day and anything else that immediately comes to mind.
5. Ask the Holy Spirit to give you light to see how you've experienced God's grace over the past day.
6. Move through the day as if you were watching it on a video. Pay attention to the feelings that your past experiences evoke.
7. Ask God for forgiveness for any sins you find yourself regretting and ask for grace to grow in love in the coming day.
8. Close with an Our Father.
9. Write about your experience of prayer.

Repeat this prayer every day for a month, and you will develop an awareness of God's work in your life. Think of ways you might adapt this prayer for your children. (See one example at the end of this chapter.)

To put it most clearly: if we don't look for God, we may not find him, but if we do look for God, he is there to be found. "You shall seek the Lord, your God; and you shall indeed find him when you search after him with your whole heart and your whole soul," writes the author of Deuteronomy (4:29; see also Is 55:6 and Mt 7:7).

Through searching for God in the everyday, we've discovered that in spite of the ways that our lives can become fragmented by the different activities and commitments that all of us are flying off to on a daily basis, family life provides ample opportunity for awareness of the slow and gentle work of God. Family life forces interruptions, often because of our children's needs: a day off from school because of sickness, a need for comfort after an injury, a desire for Mom or Dad time before bed, an opportunity for teaching after watching a TV show, and so on. Cultivating our prayer lives as parents has helped us to see those times when God is present and to use them as opportunities to weave prayer into daily life. In addition to common times like before meals or bedtime, we'll pause and pray for a moment when one of our kids needs a hug. We'll say a blessing when they wake up for school. We'll make a cross on their hands or forehead when they're heading out the door. Sometimes the prayers are to help them learn, but other times they are simply to remind ourselves to be aware of the movements of grace in daily life. They are all over the place; we just need to keep our eyes open.

Since the time when our daughters were very young, we've looked for ways to cultivate the prayer of awareness in their lives. We started with a bedtime ritual of asking three questions: What was something that made you happy today? What was something that made you sad? What are you looking forward to tomorrow? These questions aim to suggest to them that their daily lives mean something and that God is present if they learn to look for him. Similarly, at dinnertime we began the practice of "Two Things," when each family member chooses to share two things that happened over the course of the day. Like the "Three Questions" exercise, this one aims to help them treat their own life experiences as the primary place where they encounter God. By sharing these experiences with the rest of the family, then, we hope that they will come to see our domestic church as a community that helps them to know God's love more clearly.

AN EXAMEN FOR CHILDREN

1. Quiet your children before bedtime.
2. Ask them what made them happy over the past day.
3. Ask them what made them sad over the past day.
4. Ask them what they look forward to tomorrow.
5. Remind them to thank God for what made them happy, ask for God's help when they are sad, and pray for God's presence in the coming day.

CHAPTER FOUR

FAMILY LIFE AS A VOCATION

Because of the long road we had to travel to have children, we discerned how deeply rooted our shared desire for a family was. There is a theological word that expresses our most deeply held desires: *vocation*. The word comes from Latin and means "call," referring to the way that God calls us to live our lives. That is how both of us have experienced it: the desire impelled us to work together for years in order to follow this call. Early on, it was mostly a matter of survival, just trying to make ends meet while pressing on through work and school. When we did reach a point when we thought it possible to start a family, we had great hope and excitement at the prospect of welcoming a baby into our home. It seemed like the next natural step in what God had in mind when he drew us together. What really challenged our faith in God was the sense that the call had receded, that God's invitation to family life had been yanked away right at the moment when we were preparing our hearts to welcome it.

In retrospect, what is clear is that vocation must be rooted in a deeply held desire because only such a desire can give us the energy to face the inevitable obstacles life throws at us. There is an image

used in many biblical texts that captures for us what happens when
we pay attention to the deep desires of our hearts namely that of the
refiner who purifies gold or silver. Psalm 12 paints a good picture:

> The promises of the Lord are sure,
>> silver refined in a crucible,
>> silver purified seven times.

Facing difficulty in realizing our vocation to family life refined
our desires, making us ask ourselves hard questions. It was by no
means an easy time, but with the wisdom of hindsight, we can
see it was very much a graced time. We grew close to each other
because of the need to lean on each other through tests, doctor visits, recurring disappointment, and loss of hope. We had to be clear
about what we were thinking and feeling, from the small moments
of happiness in daily life to the despair we'd face with each preg-
nancy test.

Years later, when we held our daughter in our arms for the first
time, it was abundantly clear something beautiful had unfolded
in our midst during the highs and lows of our early married life.
We had been unaware of how God was moving our hearts toward
adoption, feeling only loss after heartbreaking loss. But those losses
carved out in our hearts a place where grace could creep in and nest
itself, bringing forth a new hope that was realized in the person of
a beautiful little baby.

One of our favorite images for the way God shapes our vocations is that of the sculptor who has in mind a beautiful statue. He
sees a solid block of marble and goes to work chipping away at it
with hammer and chisel. That block of marble, were it conscious of
itself, would only feel the pain of loss with each strike of the hammer until such time as it could marvel at the creation the sculptor

made. So too with us. We may feel only the loss of dreams and the crushing of desire. Faith allows us to press on, though, until the time when we can behold ourselves through the eyes with which the Sculptor sees us.

Do you ever get tired of the effort it takes to live your vocation? Do family stresses, work problems, financial concerns, health issues, and time crunches ever wear you down? Do your children (or your parents) ever drive you nuts? These feelings are certainly part of every family member's life. In our better moments, we see problems in a larger perspective, but

> ## Do I have enough faith to be able to pass it on to my kids?

sometimes these problems get the best of us. The life of prayer is above all a realistic look at the world; our favorite description is that it's "a long, loving look at the real."[3] And the reality of family life is that it is both beautiful and (oftentimes) really hard. With perspective, though, we can understand that anything worth doing—anything meaningful—is going to involve challenges. Climbing a mountain, running a marathon, studying for a degree, starting a new relationship, discovering a cure for a disease—all these things require belief in what one is doing and perseverance through the hard times. So too with family life. We are convinced that it is a life God calls people to undertake with all their energies for the sake of building his Kingdom, but it is a life that can be draining. Sometimes we need reminders of what we are working for.

> While the crowd was pressing in on Jesus and listening to the word of God, he was standing by the Lake of Gennesaret. He saw two boats there alongside the lake; the fishermen had disembarked and

were washing their nets. Getting into one of the boats, the one belonging to Simon, he asked him to put out a short distance from the shore. Then he sat down and taught the crowds from the boat. After he had finished speaking, he said to Simon, "Put out into deep water and lower your nets for a catch." Simon said in reply, "Master, we have worked hard all night and have caught nothing, but at your command I will lower the nets." When they had done this, they caught a great number of fish and their nets were tearing. They signaled to their partners in the other boat to come to help them. They came and filled both boats so that they were in danger of sinking. When Simon Peter saw this, he fell at the knees of Jesus and said, "Depart from me, Lord, for I am a sinful man." For astonishment at the catch of fish they had made seized him and all those with him, and likewise James and John, the sons of Zebedee, who were partners of Simon. Jesus said to Simon, "Do not be afraid; from now on you will be catching men." When they brought their boats to the shore, they left everything and followed him. (Lk 5:1–11)

In the story of Jesus and the fishermen, Simon and the other fishermen are exhausted after a night of fruitless fishing and have finally called it quits. Jesus suggests they give it one more try. He points them to a deep part of Lake Gennesaret where they should drop their nets, and when they do, their nets fill to bursting. Putting into the deep—trusting Jesus' words even though they feel exhausted—is the key to finding what they are after.

We have found that family life is often like that. As Christians, we believe that Jesus points toward a depth of meaning in our lives that allows us to see through the everyday to the "dearest freshness deep down things," as the poet puts it. On some level, all parents intuit this already. That grade on the math test isn't just a number; it's a third-grader's triumph. The phone call from a child's friend isn't just a small gesture of friendship; it's a sign of generosity she so desperately needs during an otherwise difficult year at school. Making the travel baseball team isn't just a summer activity; it's a truly great memory—one he'll treasure for years. And that strangely shaped clay coffee cup made by a first-grader thirty-five years ago? It's more precious than the Holy Grail.

With Kingdom eyes, family members see through ordinary realities into the deep. They understand that small gestures and small objects can carry great importance for a family's life. These things are often invested with memories that sustain family storytelling for decades. That kind of storytelling—that kind of memory—is deeply rooted in grace, for it is in a very concrete way that our relationships mirror the kind of relationship Jesus described with the Father. To use a theological term, family life is naturally *sacramental,* meaning that these concrete things can be bearers of grace, of God's love. The "ordinary" family home can be shot through with sacramental grace, reminders of abiding love that practically shout their praise to God. Understanding this truth also points to a dark side of family life: the hurts we cause one another with equally small and insignificant words and acts can cause powerful spiritual harm. A child hears a criticism and thinks Mom doesn't love her anymore; a husband carelessly leaves the room a mess, and the wife believes he no longer cares about her feelings. Family life is a font of grace, but it's also a kind of crucible where the wounds of sin can be most deeply felt.

FOSTERING GRATITUDE FOR LIFE'S JOYS

- Schedule five minutes today to pay attention to one item in your home—perhaps a toy or a picture your child has drawn—and imagine what it will mean to you in ten years. What will you miss about this stage of life?
- Start a "box of memories" with your child. Ask your child to pick something meaningful from school or an activity he or she wants to remember, and put a picture or a drawing of it in the box. Use it as an opportunity to say thank you to God.

In the deep, we listen to Christ's invitation to find what we are really looking for. The deep is the place where we learn to trust him, thereby reaping benefits we could not previously have imagined. It requires enough risk to set out from shore even when we are tired, but its payoff is a new way of appreciating family life as teeming with grace.

As parents and professionals, we have been engaged in faith formation of young people for many years. What is most clear is that the key to helping children gaze into the deep is first to deepen your own prayer life. For many, that is a daunting proposition, but we are trying to suggest that living family life reflectively is a ripe field for the cultivation of a living faith. Like many people, you may hope that your children will grow in the knowledge that God loves them, but you also hope for some guidance on how to pass on that knowledge. For many, even talking about God can be hard without falling into a language remembered from childhood. You may remember things you were taught and that you can teach your children, but along the way you may encounter new questions and doubts. We hope to encourage you to cultivate first your adult faith so that you can grow with your children in faith.

If you are like many adults, you have wrestled with your own belief in God and with the question of what to pass on to your children. Let us begin, then, with an honest admission that it is impossible to define God. At the same time, in a meaning-filled life, it is impossible to avoid God. The ancient hymn puts it most beautifully: where there is self-gift and love, God is there (*ubi caritas et amor, Deus ibi est*). For a family, God is the felt meaning when there is an overflow of emotion, the deep sense that there is incredible beauty in the world.

Our awareness of that kind of beauty, and God's presence throughout it, was heightened when we held our oldest daughter for the first time. The world opened up; we could see clearly that we would live for this child in a way that made our previous life feel small. We became conscious of our limitations, as if the usual sense of confidence with which we approached the world yielded to a humility about how best to care for this child. Our world changed; the old certainties faded away. We needed to develop an understanding of the usual parenting tasks: care and feeding, emotional attachment, education and formation, and so on. We could catch glimpses of the future: negotiating questions about school, sports, religion, music, work, and all the rest of what parents face in raising their children. We were awestruck and more than a little afraid. But at the same time, we were deeply in love—in love with this beautiful child, in love with each other for our mutual willingness to take on this life together. And in that coexistence of terror and love, we sensed God as he passed by.

The Psalmist wrote, "the fear of the Lord is the beginning of wisdom" (Ps 111:10). That poetic statement captures for us the kind of feeling that emerged in our first experience of parenting, and it made what we had learned about prayer as children begin to make more sense. We pray because we are human, and yet we hope to love the way only God can. The meaningful moments in life make us aware of our limitations, of our inability to fully control those things that move us most deeply. We can be melted by beauty or devastated by grief, and both experiences can make us acutely aware of our smallness. Yet the human heart is resilient; it continues to reach out in love for answers. We pray in part because we want to reach out, to discover if in that reaching out there might be someone else reaching to meet us. What is remarkable about family life is that it is almost by its very definition a suspension of selfish desire in favor of a constant, pioneering search for shared joy. Entering into marriage with a hope of a lifetime friendship with another person is certainly an act of faith because it involves the constant negotiation of personal desire ("I want"), shared desire ("we want"), and sacrificial desire ("I want what you want"). How much more an act of faith, then, is entrance into family life, in which a person or a couple also consents to enter into the messy, creative, unpredictable, surprising world of children!

> **God is in the direction of our deepest hopes rooted in love.**

Regardless of how you have experienced family life, though—whether through careful planning or by accident, through marriage or through other kinds of relationships, whether with joy or with fear and uncertainty—you are in the midst of a life's work that involves many acts of faith. And these acts of faith, of uncertainty, are rooted in the hopes you have for yourself and your loved ones. Perhaps one way to conceive of God is to consider the direction of our deepest hopes rooted in love. Perhaps the answer to why we pray is that it is how we practice imagining the way that God can love. Perhaps God is the origin and goal of what we most deeply desire for the ones we love.

Yet if we thought God showed up only at those times of emotional high, it would be tough to consider him a friend. What if it were a time of suffering? What if God sat back, like in the book of Job, and let Satan afflict his servants with every manner of plague and distress? We have friends who, when faced with a terrible family tragedy, blamed it all on God and walked out of church for the rest of their lives. If God is supposed to deliver peak experiences but sends pain instead, how are we to view that God as worthy of our prayer? And if we cannot come to a satisfactory answer as to whether God is "worthy," how then do we persevere?

We persevere in prayer because we trust in the examples of those who have shown us how to live wisely, to believe in the words and actions of Jesus as showing us something deeply true and real about what it means to be human and to love. Prayer does not necessarily give us peak experiences, nor can it shelter us from suffering. Rather, it helps us to see both peak experiences and suffering with the long view, seeing them as moments in a much longer story. That story is about God making a world and putting us in it, about giving us desires that are designed to lead us to a life's purpose, and about finding joy in fulfilling it in our family life. It's a story about how we often confuse those great desires with simple and easily fulfilled desires like a child who spoils his dinner by eating too much candy. It's a story about growing up in wisdom, discerning the difference between great and small desires, and finding people who share the great ones. The story continues in the life we build, making decisions about money, time, work, religion, family, children, sex, recreation, health, and old age. In this story, Jesus emerges as a guide and leader, hoping to point us toward great desires that make our lives meaningful. And like any good and wise guide, he is capable of helping us navigate the storms, rough ground, accidents, and even tragedies that befall us on our pilgrimage. He points us toward God because he was God among us.

Thankfully, this is a God who has taught us how to live both as individuals and as members of families. In the next several chapters, we'll explore the six rules that have emerged from the Christian tradition and how these rules can help us both as adults and as those charged with helping form young people in love.

PART TWO

RULES FOR FAMILY SPIRITUALITY

CHAPTER FIVE

THE FIRST RULE: GOD BRINGS OUR FAMILY TOGETHER ON PILGRIMAGE

There are two common ways of making a journey and two common ways of making a life.

The first way is to wander, taking in the interesting things along the way. There will be highs and lows, good times and bad, but eventually it's over. The cliché "life is a journey, not a destination" points to this way. The film icon of this "journey life" is Forrest Gump, whose observation "life is like a box of chocolates. You never know what you're going to get" suggests that an openness to the wonder of life can lead us to opportunities we could never plan. But this approach might also be aimless, hiding a fear of going after worthy goals, dissuading us from taking on great challenges for the sake of building a better world. Parents who teach this way of living are more likely to ensure that their children are having fun and less likely to challenge them to undertake great things for others.

The second way is to have your eyes fixed on where you are going, to be eager about getting there, and to structure your passage accordingly. There may be interesting things along the way, and there may be obstacles, but the key is to arrive. This approach to life is different; it regards cultural trends with some suspicion, as they may distract us from our destination. Practically speaking, those who have their eyes set on a destination tend to be very focused on what helps them get there, and such individuals have little time for anything else. The father in *Dead Poets Society* was driven, and he drove his son toward a perceived good. Of course, the quality of the "destination life" depends on the quality of the destination, the perceived good. Olympic athletes, CEOs, and others can live "destination lives" very successfully. But others who become driven may miss out on the simple joys of everyday life.

There is a middle way, though: the way of pilgrimage. The Jewish philosopher Martin Buber hinted at this way in his observation that "all journeys have secret destinations of which the traveler is unaware." The Rules for Family Spirituality we are going to lay out suggest this way of pilgrimage: God brings us together for a purpose, and our life's work is to learn it and live it. Along the way, there are abundant challenges but also abundant graces, such that we can both take delight in the journey yet still move with purpose toward our destination, eternal life. The way of pilgrimage is an act of faith, to be sure—but let's observe that any way of living (for the atheist as much as for the Christian) is an act of faith, inasmuch as it involves making decisions about how to live in the face of uncertainty. The rules are about acting according to the faith taught by Jesus, mindful that at the very least it is a faith that has been practiced by many before and involves the promise that the One in whom we place this faith walks along with us on the pilgrimage.

The pilgrimage life is one of both journey and destination. First, it is a life of purpose: it involves the belief that we can orchestrate all our talents, desires, inclinations, even weaknesses into a beautiful harmony for the sake of God's Kingdom. It rests in the words of Psalm 139, which speak to each member of the family:

> You formed my inmost being;
>> you knit me in my mother's womb.
>> I praise you, because I am wonderfully made.

It is a life in which we profess faith in a God who has numbered the hairs on our head (Mt 10:30), who has created us to work on his unfolding project, his Kingdom. Blessed John Henry Newman's prayer exemplifies this approach:

> God has created me to do Him some definite service; He has committed some work to me which He has not committed to another. I have my mission—I never may know it in this life, but I shall be told it in the next. Somehow I am necessary for His purposes, as necessary in my place as an Archangel in his—if, indeed, I fail, He can raise another, as He could make the stones children of Abraham. Yet I have a part in this great work; I am a link in a chain, a bond of connection between persons. He has not created me for naught. I shall do good, I shall do His work; I shall be an angel of peace, a preacher of truth in my own place, while not intending it, if I do but keep His commandments and serve Him in my calling.
>
> Therefore I will trust Him. Whatever, wherever I am, I can never be thrown away. If I am in sickness,

> my sickness may serve Him; in perplexity, my per-
> plexity may serve Him; if I am in sorrow, my sorrow
> may serve Him. My sickness, or perplexity, or sorrow
> may be necessary causes of some great end, which is
> quite beyond us. He does nothing in vain; He may
> prolong my life, He may shorten it; He knows what
> He is about. He may take away my friends, He may
> throw me among strangers, He may make me feel
> desolate, make my spirits sink, hide the future from
> me—still He knows what He is about.[4]

As a life of purpose, the pilgrimage life is a life oriented toward the "here and now" of building the Kingdom. Unlike following an established blueprint a Divine Architect has drawn, the pilgrimage life is more like bringing together God's people: it involves working cooperatively with God to form relationships of authentic love with the whole human family. So there is at once an awareness of the destination (unity among people, giving thanks and praise to God) as well as a practical interest in the beauty of the journey.

The pilgrimage life, like pilgrimage itself, is about surprises along the way. Historically, people have understood pilgrimages as microcosms of life itself: one journeys toward a destination, but along the way one experiences surprises and conversions. The recent film *The Way* is an example. Tom Avery, an American ophthalmologist whose son has died on the medieval pilgrimage route El Camino de Santiago, goes to retrieve his son's belongings. Once there, he decides he will undertake the pilgrimage in his son's place. He is not sure about God; he is not sure about why he undertakes the pilgrimage or what he will find at the end. But he finds many surprises along the way, and he arrives in Santiago de Compostela a changed man.

In our own life, the way of pilgrimage has led us in directions we could never have imagined at the beginning of our marriage. Once upon a time, we had a five-year plan. We discovered—within about a year or two—that the plan was not going to happen! The most recent lesson has been the adoption of our son, an eight-year-old. The decision was not something we had explicitly planned; rather, it emerged in our prayer as something we felt God was calling us to do. At the time of this writing, we are celebrating three months home with him, having begun the process just over a year ago. Just a few months prior to that, we did not anticipate adopting again, thinking the needs of our daughters and the strain on our finances was just too much to consider more kids.

What made the decision happen? First, we knew each other well and knew that had there been no serious obstacles, we would have already adopted again. We had come to discover so many graces through our parenting—graces that were wrought out of many struggles, to be sure, but which (because of those same struggles) surprised us with their beauty. Second, we were committed to facing the existing struggles in our family life, and we asked hard questions about what bringing another child into the family might mean. We had to talk about it with our daughters and communicate that the experience would teach them lessons of sharing, forgiveness, and responsibility. Third, we knew that the desire to adopt was rooted in deeper desires to be loving and generous, and we could see this desire was in harmony with our understanding of the kind of life Jesus modeled. Eventually, we made the decision that adopting again—which would entail sacrifice and massive change in our family life—was a necessary part of the pilgrimage we were walking with God. The road we once looked down has now changed, but the pilgrimage continues.

The pilgrimage life need not be at first a life of absolute certainty about God, about Jesus, about the Church, or about prayer. It need only be a willingness to begin and a hope that in undertaking the pilgrimage, one's life will be a life of both purpose and surprises that God can orchestrate for the sake of symphonic harmony with the rest of creation.

What does this all mean, practically speaking? The rules of a family's spiritual life rest upon the willingness of the parents to live this pilgrimage life. It means, for example,

- Taking a leadership role. Each parent is willing to talk honestly about his or her questions about God, Jesus, the Church, about his or her religious upbringing, his or her understanding of prayer. It means that each parent is willing to share the pilgrimage with the rest of the family and not assume that someone else (a spouse, the kids' grandparents or teachers) will take care of the kids' spiritual lives.

- Practicing the spiritual life. If spirituality is to be more than an intellectual exercise, it has to involve concrete action. This may mean grace before meals, a family prayer sometime during the day, shared public worship (going to Church), or a commitment to social action like serving in a homeless shelter. Whatever the practice, it must be actively shared by parents and children. We'll talk more about practices throughout this book and offer specific ones to cultivate the spiritual lives of both parents and children. (See the appendix for a list.)

- Learning from those who are wise. No one can automatically claim expertise in medicine, financial planning, construction, or gardening without learning from those who've been at those things for a long time. So too with spirituality. Seek out those who pray, teach, serve, counsel, or lead worship, and plan to be challenged. Seek out experts, read their books, speak with others, and teach what you learn to your children.

To say that God brings our family together on pilgrimage is not to say that we as parents give up our freedom or that somehow we are just acting according to some preordained fate. Instead, it is saying that when we act in love as a family, God is very much there, walking with us toward a future full of hope. It also suggests that the pilgrimage itself will involve negotiating things we do not expect, but the process of doing so is itself fraught with grace. Over time, what becomes clear is that the journey itself does not exhaust meaning, nor does the destination. Love finds the balance between them—and to this point we now turn.

CHAPTER SIX

THE SECOND RULE: OUR LOVE FOR ONE ANOTHER LEADS TO JOY

In the context of the Christian spiritual tradition, family life is a vocation, a calling, a fundamental choice about how to live out one's pilgrimage life. It is a particular role within the Body of Christ, which is to say that it represents a specific way of serving the world. Family life is always a public life, inasmuch as the members of the family intersect with the world in many ways: school, sports, work, clubs and organizations, and so on.

What the rules propose is that the life of following Jesus is about living purposefully, and a particular way of doing that is by learning how to love the members of our families. To say it a bit differently, the purposeful life is always about imitating God by pouring out our lives in love, and family love is a privileged vocation.

To echo an earlier point, practicing this vocation means actively seeking to learn it in the context of doing it. What makes this task difficult is that we've seen a breakdown in models of family life in recent decades: there's not much agreement on how to parent well. Older parents, psychologists, spiritual guides, economists, teachers, coaches, and many others may have wisdom to contribute, but in the end, each parent must develop the desire to improve his or her understanding of what it means to parent within the unique circumstances of one's family. Thomas Merton's famous prayer might be helpful as a reminder of cultivating this desire.

> My Lord God, I have no idea where I am going. I do not see the road ahead of me. I cannot know for certain where it will end. Nor do I really know myself, and the fact that I think I am following your will does not mean that I am actually doing so. But I believe that the desire to please you does in fact please you. And I hope I have that desire in all that I am doing. I hope that I will never do anything apart from that desire. And I know that if I do this you will lead me by the right road, though I may know nothing about it. Therefore I will trust you always though I may seem to be lost and in the shadow of death. I will not fear, for you are ever with me, and you will never leave me to face my perils alone.[5]

This is a prayer that most parents can pray easily because it captures the inherent uncertainty of our vocation. We simply cannot know everything there is to know about parenting well, and so we are frequently left to our own confusion in sorting out how to proceed.

We've been deeply moved by the stories of parents close to us who have had to negotiate difficult questions about how to parent children with special needs. We've seen moms and dads who have had to move heaven and earth to get proper educational services, medical care, or psychological testing. At every stage, there are experts who can cite studies and point to the state of knowledge within their disciplines, yet parents have had to fall back on the recognition that their child is not "the state of the discipline," but a unique individual whom they themselves have come to know best. One mom very dear to us, for example, put on hold a teaching career to focus full-time on her autistic son who had significant speech delays. She holds a prestigious advanced degree and worked for a number of years both in the classroom and in the training of teachers to use technology in their work. But what recently has taken her time and energy is a passion to help her son develop the ability to speak and read. He has learned those things but not without massive efforts by his mother to advocate for him at every stage of his development.

The 1993 film *Lorenzo's Oil* tells the true story of Lorenzo Odone, whose parents (Augusto and Michaela) struggle to find a cure for the obscure disease afflicting their son. In real life, their efforts against adrenoleukodystrophy (ALD) yielded the discovery of a mixture of rapeseed and olive oils that helped certain people afflicted with the disorder. The film, nominated for two Academy awards, shows in dramatic fashion the lengths to which the couple goes in advocating for their son. It is a remarkable story of what real love can summon from those who embrace a vocation to parenting.

Most parents, of course, are exempt from the kinds of challenges the film portrays, yet all parents face challenges in learning how to really love the members of their families. Love is demanding; it involves paying close attention to the beloved, spending time with him or her, and looking for opportunities to help seek his or her good. The rules propose that the whole process of paying attention, spending time with those we love, seeking out ways of serving their good, being stretched in our time and patience and abilities—all these things are shot through with grace. Recalling that our very life's purpose is loving our families, we are emphasizing that there need not be a "my, this feels holy!" feeling all the time. Quite the contrary: it may be frustrating, debilitating, boring, or stressful at times, while at others it may be exhilarating, peaceful, empowering, or reassuring at others. As a pilgrimage, family life will involve highs and lows along the way that we do well to stop and reflect on. But it also will involve moving along the pilgrimage, mindful that, in the end, it is the way we are achieving eternal life. It will involve moments of doubt and darkness as well as moments of crystal clarity, as if the fabric between heaven and earth has been stretched so as to become translucent.

CHAPTER SEVEN

THE THIRD RULE: OUR FAMILY DOESN'T CARE ABOUT "SUCCESS"

Not long ago, a family we know experienced the death of a daughter, a baby girl whose birth the family was anticipating with great joy and excitement. In their generosity, the family invited members of our daughter's school to the funeral Mass to celebrate the life of their beloved little girl. It was a beautiful and moving ceremony, one that stuck with our daughters and raised important topics for our own family's conversation.

What strikes us as we remember that Mass is the fact that the family treated it as both a sadness and a joy. Any death, no matter how young the person, is an occasion for mourning the loss of what that person brought (or could have brought) into the world. Yet in the Christian life, it is also an occasion for joy: a recognition that God has graced us with the gift and responsibility of another's life and that the person is already a gift before he or she does anything.

It is sometimes easy to focus on obvious negatives (sickness, poverty, death) because we quickly jump to thinking about what is lacking (health, wealth, long life). What the rules propose, though, is that there is freedom in coming to see reality on its own terms rather than on terms we impose from our small imaginations. Our friends' baby lived nestled in her mother's womb for many months. What a beautiful and peaceful image! What a gift to the entire family! The fact that the girl died shortly after being born need not compromise the grace that she was to the family. Similarly, other struggles in our lives arise because of expectations about *what is supposed to be* rather than dwelling in appreciation of *what really is*.

> Spiritual freedom is a prerequisite for openness to the creativity of love.

This kind of appreciation for reality is about achieving spiritual freedom. Small desires can hamstring our willingness to love; they can get in the way of our acting in generosity. To be unconcerned with having lots of money, for example, is to be free from forming unhealthy desires that can compromise our family's flourishing. It's a way of saying, "We'll be a happy family whether we're rich or poor. We'll love one other either way." Similarly, being unattached to health or sickness means "we'll love one another whether we're healthy or sick." Indifference toward a long life or a short one means "we'll love one another whether it's for ten minutes or ten decades." This kind of spiritual freedom is a prerequisite for openness to the creativity of love.

During our last trip to China, we met a family whose story is a parable of this kind of positive indifference. Scott and Kathy Rosenow started a family with the same hopes as anyone else, but two of their four biological children had significant special needs.

Witnessing how the children benefitted from each other's presence, the Rosenows asked how they might share this kind of benefit with other children with special needs. Remarkably, they did not first ask the practical questions (How much will this cost? Is our home big enough? How can we save for college? Will the other kids feel squeezed?). In a spirit of indifference, they simply asked, "What does God want?" The answer: "more." Over the next several years, they adopted no fewer than seventeen children from China, Haiti, Bolivia, Guatemala, Ukraine, and Romania—all with some kind of special need. What initially seemed to be obstacles, such as money, time, and physical space, they eventually overcame. They are a family on a mission to build a Kingdom of love right at home.[6]

The Rosenows are free people. They don't care what others think of their choices; they don't care what cars they drive or how well-appointed their house happens to be. Nor are they concerned with the usual markers of success for their children—ability on the playing field or grades in school. Their great desire is to give needy children a home and a family.

Greg Boyle, S.J., a Jesuit priest who founded Homeboy Industries to minister to former gang members in East Los Angeles, has written movingly about the kind of spiritual freedom the Rosenows and countless other families manifest in their lives. He raises questions about whether our desire for success is, in the long run, a good thing.

> Jesus was always too busy being faithful to worry about success. I'm not opposed to success; I just think we should accept it only if it is a by-product of our fidelity. If our primary concern is results, we will choose to work only with those who give us good ones.[7]

The third rule proposes that we throw away whatever we imagine success to look like, because that vision is likely the product of what we've absorbed from popular culture. Instead, with spiritual freedom we gain the ability to be surprised by happiness. We think less about what we don't have, and we are able to marvel in what is unfolding right before us.

Some years ago, one of our daughters was having problems with sleep. Even at eight years old, she could not sleep through the night and would come into our bedroom to wake us up, asking if she could sleep with us. Dealing with that problem on a daily basis was absolutely exhausting and caused no small amount of frustration. It was damaging our relationship with her because as we became irritable, we would sometimes speak angrily to her about needing to sleep. At a certain point, though, it was clear that this sleep issue was not going away and was likely rooted in some fears she had developed while at the orphanage. Accepting that truth, rather than trying to discipline her for the behavior, opened us to a new way of looking at the problem. Rather than seeing the night-time wake-ups as interruptions, we began to recognize that when she experienced fear, she came to us for comfort. We were the voice of calm, of safety, of love for her—everything she lacked while in the orphanage. We saw that neither adequate nor inadequate sleep changed our purpose: to love her through the pains of nightmares so that she could eventually grow past them.

Achieving spiritual freedom often follows the pattern of what we learned in that process. We came to see that one desire (for sleep) was slowly displaced by a deeper and more profound desire (to love her through her fears). What made that lesson possible was the willingness not to fixate on what appeared to be an immediate good. It was not an easy lesson, but it was incredibly important.

(Over time, by the way, she did learn to sleep on her own without fear.)

The third rule invites us to question what we think is good, to ask whether our vision of what's good is ultimately in service to an expansive and generous love. If it is not, then it is also an invitation to let go of that vision, so a newer one might grow in its place.

CHAPTER EIGHT

THE FOURTH RULE: GOD STRETCHES OUR FAMILY TOWARD HIS KINGDOM

When Jesus used the words "God" and "Kingdom," he knew his listeners shared a Jewish worldview and therefore could make connections to stories they had learned from the scriptures. It is impossible today to recapture all the nuances of that Jewish worldview; for that, we recommend learning as much as you can about the history, language, celebrations, and symbols of the Old Testament because that world was the world Jesus himself lived in. It gave him the language of prayer. (A great gift that Jews today continue to give us is the gathered wisdom of that long tradition of worshipping God.)[8]

The world is different today, though, and so we want to suggest what it means to say today that God calls us to build his Kingdom. First, who is God? You may be calling to mind the things you learned in religious education or old images you had as a child: the old man with the white beard, the Creator of the universe, love.

Most people have some way of giving words to their understanding of God, but in our experience, many have a problem communicating their ideas when their children inevitably ask them the question of who God is or where the world came from. What do you want your children to understand?

What the rules propose is that God is the name we give to a Person who loves us by calling us into being and giving meaning to our lives. God is the origin and direction of our most authentic selves, the author and object of our most authentic desires, the reality we experience directly when we are seized by love and compelled by beauty. Can we "prove" God? Probably not—if by "proof" we mean something we can easily grasp by the intellect, by reasoning from effects to causes. But then we can't "prove" that we love each other that way either. Proof is the result of using the intellect as a tool for certain tasks; faith is the action of an entire life in the face of mysteries that defy the use of the tool of the intellect. The best we can do is remove the obstacles to belief in God and recognize that faith nestles within us in a different location from our thinking, closer to the places where our emotions, our passions, and our music reside. It is less helpful to speak of "belief in God," which connotes something our brains do, and more helpful to speak of "faith in God," which is something our

> God is the origin and direction of our most authentic selves, the author and object of our most authentic desires, the reality we experience directly when we are seized by love and compelled by beauty.

hearts compel us to do whether we are thinking about it or not. Belief is what we think; faith is how we live.

Children live faithfully in an unselfconscious way. They experience wonder at the world; they express love and affection; they strive to learn; they grow and develop and ask questions. Theirs is a world imbued with purpose and meaning. Our first task as parents is to help them name that meaning and reflect upon it. To their question, "Who is God?" perhaps you might answer along these lines.

> God is the one who made everything. God is who made you able to ask questions. God is there when you feel happy and who reminds you things will be better when you feel sad. God made you able to grow and learn to love and make friends. God is who brings happiness to those who have pain, who hugs people who have died, who heals people even though their bodies may be sick. God moves us to do great things out of love. God is who keeps reminding us to become good and beautiful and who never gives up on us.

The Bible gives us language for God and is helpful for our growth as people of faith. Jesus, who masterfully used parables to describe God, frequently returned to an analogy that has been at the heart of Christian theology for centuries: the "Kingdom." In many places throughout the gospels (more than one hundred times), Jesus describes an unfolding of the reality of God in our midst by using the term "Kingdom." At face value, the idea is pretty clear: God's in charge like a benevolent ruler, and we're his subjects. But on a deeper level, what we see in Jesus' descriptions of the Kingdom is a complex commentary on the ordinary ways people interact and a promise that in learning how to love one another, we are helping to bring about a more perfect world. Consider, for example, the Beatitudes, so named because they describe how to be happy or blessed (*beatus* in Latin):

> Blessed are the poor in spirit, for theirs is the kingdom of heaven.
> Blessed are they who mourn, for they will be comforted.
> Blessed are the meek, for they will inherit the land.
> Blessed are they who hunger and thirst for righteousness, for they will be satisfied.
> Blessed are the merciful, for they will be shown mercy.
> Blessed are the clean of heart, for they will see God.
> Blessed are the peacemakers, for they will be called children of God.
> Blessed are they who are persecuted for the sake of righteousness, for theirs is the kingdom of heaven. (Mt 5:3–10)

These counterintuitive statements suggest this Kingdom is different from our usual way of looking at things, but our participation in it will lead to our happiness or blessedness. In the context of family life, it is compelling to imagine what these ideas about the Kingdom might mean.

Primarily, the Kingdom looks like a place where none of us is the center of the universe: that place is reserved for God. As much as families almost demand a certain measure of selflessness, still it can be easy to fall into patterns of assuming others are there to serve us and our happiness. Not so, suggest the Beatitudes: happiness arrives not as something we pursue for its own sake; rather, it arrives softly while we are busy at the work of loving one another.

Take, for one example, the seventh Beatitude describing peacemakers as "children of God." How often do parents find themselves taking on this role among their children? How often do you find yourself practically shrieking at your children to stop fighting and be nice? If you're like us, you don't particularly relish those moments, though on some level, you know they are absolutely necessary if children are to avoid growing into monsters. The seventh Beatitude doesn't appear at face value to be the easy recipe for quiet contentment on the level, say, of sipping iced tea on a lanai overlooking a Hawaiian sunset. Being a peacemaker wouldn't exactly merit mention in the list of "100 Things to Do Before You Die"

> Happiness arrives not as something we pursue for its own sake; rather, it arrives softly while we are busy at the work of loving one another.

next to visiting the Grand Canyon. Quite the contrary: being a peacemaker at home can be understood only as a means to a greater end, namely having a loving family and training your children to be active participants in it. The Beatitudes as a whole are fundamentally goal oriented: they point us toward a picture of happiness beyond the present moment.

On some level, every parent understands this dimension of Kingdom-building. Welcoming children into a family means signing up for all kinds of stresses amidst many kinds of joys. No parent can rationally assume family life is all about moving from one happy moment to the next. There is naturally a sense of building for the long term and drawing meaning from the ups and downs of family life in the hope love will prevail.

We realize the Kingdom every time we act in love. We delay the Kingdom every time hopelessness overcomes us or every time we refuse to make the hard decisions love often demands. Family life stretches us—our patience, our tolerance for stress, our willingness to sacrifice. But it also stretches our hearts, making them more flexible and agile in the work of love. When we are living family life well, we are bringing forth God's Kingdom.

CHAPTER NINE

THE FIFTH RULE:
GOD WILL HELP US

Jesus said, "Ask and it will be given to you; seek and you will find; knock and the door will be opened to you" (Mt 7:7). God does not overpower us or take away our freedom to make choices, but—like us, when our children ask us for something we want them to have—God longs to help us when we act in freedom for the Kingdom.

Not long ago, one of our daughters asked for a book that all her friends had been reading. She wanted to know what all the fuss was about and to be part of the conversation. She was a little surprised when, the next day, we ran out to the bookstore to buy it for her. To us, it was simple. We had been trying to encourage her to read more, and this seemed like an obvious way to do it. She had become used to hearing "no" to repeated requests to watch TV or a movie, which we tried to tell her was about wanting her not to have too much screen time over the course of a week. She was pleasantly surprised to receive such a quick response to her wish.

God works in a similar way. Our desires to work for the Kingdom are good and holy desires. They may not always be the best way to bring forth the Kingdom; it takes a lifetime to practice discerning where God is moving our hearts. But Jesus promises that God gives us what we need to serve the purpose for which God has created us, if we learn to ask for it.

> Ask and it will be given to you; seek and you will
> find; knock and the door will be opened to you.
> (Mt 7:7)

There is a difficult corollary to this point, though: sometimes we don't get what we ask for, and that can be painful. It can be especially painful when what we ask for appears obviously good to us, such as health for ourselves or our children. The most challenging dimension of faith is that to be real, it must challenge whatever understandings of happiness we currently hold—as Jesus suggested in his Beatitudes. Most people develop understandings of happiness by looking at people around them, to the extent that we tend to measure our happiness in terms of what we lack and what others have. That, according to Jesus, is not a good yardstick. Rather, we ought to measure our happiness according to the unique purpose for which God has made us.

The hardest period in our early married life was when we kept hearing "no" to our desire to conceive a child. We had talked about welcoming children into our home, and we both felt convicted that we were called to the vocation of marriage in large part because of our shared desire for children. So it was no small challenge to run up against wall after wall in the process of trying to conceive—in fact, it felt like God had abandoned us. The period of struggling through infertility was an experience of desolation, and it forced us to ask very basic questions about how well we understood what God had created us for. We knew couples whose relationships had been lacerated by the stress of infertility, and that scared us. Were we just fooling ourselves?

What preserved our sanity throughout this period was constant communication. More specifically, it was learning new ways of communicating so that we did not let the other person feel he or she was suffering alone. Our faith told us God would never abandon us, and though some days it certainly felt that way, one thing that remained constant was our dedication to show love to each other. We developed a new appreciation for the idea that marriage is a sacrament—a visible sign of the deep love God lavishes on people—because of the ways we managed to love each other through the low (and even lower) points.

Over time, what emerged as a result of God effectively saying "no" to the desire to conceive children was a profound and beautiful desire to adopt. One desire had to die in order for the other to grow. We have seen this pattern time and again both in our own lives and in the lives of friends. To put it simply, God gives us what we need to serve our purpose, and sometimes what we most need is the pruning of one desire so that another may blossom.

> It is God asking,
>   "Can you trust that
> I am with you
>   when life is hard
>   and that I will help
> steer you toward
>   a more lasting
> happiness if you
> let go of what you think
> will make you happy?"

The fifth rule is, in one sense, a test of faith. It's the question, "Are you willing to stay the course even though the seas may be rough?" It is God asking, "Can you trust that I am with you when life is hard and that I will help steer you toward a more lasting happiness if you let go of what you think will make you happy?" It's a lesson both for parents and children.

When one of our daughters was very young, we told her the story of how to trap a monkey. The story goes that you can trap a monkey by putting a banana in a jar whose mouth is just wide enough for the monkey's hand to fit through. The monkey will reach in and grab the banana, but it will become stuck because that hand clutching the banana will be too wide to come back out. The desire for the banana will be so strong that the monkey will not let it go, even if it means becoming trapped.

Nowadays, that image of the monkey clutching the banana is shorthand in our home for holding on to desires that trap us. "Drop the banana!" we'll say in the midst of a tantrum. Perhaps she sees her brother getting something she wants, or she hears "no" to an unreasonable request for a TV show in the midst of chores. She may not see the larger goods we want for her; she perceives only that her parents are denying her something she wants. So too with God: the fifth rule suggests to us that even as adults we do not always see what God is laboring to create in us. Like a good parent—an image used frequently in the Bible—God wants to help us live the purpose for which he has made us, even when we don't understand it.

CHAPTER TEN

THE SIXTH RULE:
WE MUST LEARN WHICH DESIRES
LEAD US TO FREEDOM

It can be very hard to understand which of our desires need pruning and which need cultivating. This is a challenge adults face in both their own lives and in their vocation as parents.

Consider for a moment all the choices you face in a day, both for yourself and for your children: when to get out of bed; what to eat for breakfast; what the day's schedule will look like; what to wear; whether to spend time cleaning up around the house or helping your children do it themselves; how and when to get to school or work or a friend's house or the supermarket or the library; what to do about lunch or dinner; how to prioritize tasks; how to ensure your child is learning spelling, grammar, math, history, a foreign language, a sport, good manners, compassion toward others, and so on. There is an endless list of priorities! How do we decide which priorities demand our time and attention? How do we decide which ones are worth desiring and which ones are just a drain on our time?

Moreover, how do we learn to pass on our priorities to our children—say, eating more vegetables than processed, sugary foods?

From the earliest centuries of Christianity (and even earlier among other philosophers East and West), there emerged an understanding of a paradox at the heart of human nature: we often desire things that are bad for us. It seems unique to human beings—animals, for the most part, eat only what their bodies need, and they tend to avoid deep-fried candy bars and reality TV. Saint Paul put it most starkly: "What I do, I do not understand. For I do not do what I want, but I do what I hate" (Rom 7:15). Why is that?

> What I do,
> I do not understand.
> For I do not do what I
> want, but I do what I hate.
> ROMANS 7:15

The answer points to something at the very root of the Christian understanding of what it means to be a human being: God has created us to be free. An implication of this understanding is that we are responsible for "managing" our desires. We use the word "managing" because it is suggestive of the task of choosing how to use them rather than of creating them from scratch. We don't really create our desires; they seem to be part of our basic programming, so to speak, by virtue of the way God has made us. From a scientific perspective, that's a way of saying that the complexities of DNA make it possible for there to be different balances of traits in different people. From a theological perspective, though, it's simply an acknowledgement that no one really creates him- or herself; the best we can do is take what we have and use it well or badly.

Parents can intuit this truth by watching their children. The parents at our daughters' schools have found any number of activities for their children to try: sewing, soccer, basketball, piano, various languages, science or math camp, swimming, softball or baseball, guitar, dance, gymnastics, and so on. And the banter around the various fields, gyms, and classrooms tends to revolve around what so-and-so is good at, what he or she detests, and what he or she will be signed up for next summer. Many parents have ideas of the kind of young people their children are developing into: perhaps a soccer star who is good at math, a baseball player who can speak Spanish, or a piano player who is good at creative writing. Maybe if they are particularly ambitious, the parents already have an eye on their future doctor or lawyer and want to ensure they are preparing their kids for college applications.

> A desire that makes us unfree is a desire that does not help us toward the end for which God has created us.

Both of us have spent most of our adult lives working with students from grammar school through college, and we've seen both the benefits of cultivating young people's talents as well as the fallout from parents forcing them to pursue life goals their children find stifling. To use the language of the rules we've proposed, what we see is that some young people have discovered desires that lead them to love, while others have felt trapped by desires that make them unfree. Simply put, a desire that makes us unfree is a desire that does not help us toward the end for which God has created us. It may be a desire for a good thing—say, a career in medicine. But not everyone is made for a medical career, and so pursuing it can be toxic to some young people. Having advised many college students over the years, we have often had to help students come to realize that their dreams of being a doctor are really their parents' dreams and that the D they got in chemistry might be an indicator that their real desires lie elsewhere. We've seen students try to push themselves, doing psychological harm (sometimes physical harm because they stay up too late studying) by pursuing a false desire.

A goal of the spiritual life is to learn how to recognize the signs that a desire is either good and worthy of pursuing or distracting and worth overcoming. This goal is intimately related to the first rule: God has made us a

> ## The goal of the spiritual life is to be ourselves.

certain way, and so our task is not to create ourselves based on somebody else's template (be it our notion of success or beauty or whatever) but rather to pay attention to what God has done by creating us. Simply put, the goal of the spiritual life, both for ourselves and our children, is to be ourselves.

Remember Hans Christian Andersen's story *The Ugly Duckling?* It's about a young swan who grows up among ducks and who, at every turn, thinks he is inferior because he is not like the ducks. The standard by which he measures himself is inadequate and twists his self-understanding so that he is unable to understand what kind of a creature he really is—until he finally meets other swans who accept him for who he is. Sometimes the world our children live in (not to mention the world we often find ourselves in) has that kind of effect: it teaches them to desire things that do not allow their most real selves to flourish. Our role as parents is to help them name those false desires, so that they might discover more deeply rooted authentic desires that will help them grow into the people God has created them to be.

In the coming chapters, we'll explore the wisdom of the Christian tradition to find ideas about how to do exactly that in our vocation as parents.

PRAYING THE RULES

You have created our family for a purpose: to praise and serve you through the way we love one another as a family. Help us not to lose sight of that purpose. Help us find you in financial trouble, stress at work or school, sickness, or even death. Help us to find joy in our daily lives together and to build your Kingdom of justice and love and mercy and beauty together. Help us learn to celebrate the coming of your Kingdom right at home. And please help us come to desire you and all the things that bring about your Kingdom, and help us to let go of the small desires that hold us back from becoming free.

PART **THREE**

PRAYING AND LIVING THE RULES

CHAPTER ELEVEN

SACRED STORIES

> [Jesus said] "How many times I yearned to gather your children together as a hen gathers her brood under her wings. . . ." (Lk 13:34)

The gospels are filled with images of parents and children, brothers and sisters, husbands and wives, and people who are single through divorce or widowhood. The world Jesus lived in was in many ways like our own in the importance people placed upon family relationships, so it is no surprise that Jesus taught images of family as ways of drawing people into deeper understanding of the Kingdom of God. One of the most unassuming yet telling of these passages is in the tenth chapter of Mark's gospel, where Jesus describes people wanting to bring their children to Jesus so he might touch them.

> And people were bringing children to him that he might touch them, but the disciples rebuked them. When Jesus saw this he became indignant and said to them, "Let the children come to me; do not prevent them, for the kingdom of God belongs to such as

these. Amen, I say to you, whoever does not accept the kingdom of God like a child will not enter it." Then he embraced them and blessed them, placing his hands on them. (Mk 10:13–16)

The story begins with the observation that people were drawn to Jesus. What had they heard? What were the testimonies of their friends and acquaintances like? Perhaps some of these people lived in the same neighborhood as a man named Jairus, whom Mark introduces in chapter 5. Mark describes him as a synagogue official, but we don't know much about him except for the fact that he loved his daughter, who was gravely ill.

Seeing [Jesus] he fell at his feet and pleaded earnestly with him, saying, "My daughter is at the point of death. Please, come lay your hands on her that she may get well and live." He went off with him, and a large crowd followed him and pressed upon him. (Mk 5:22–24)

We can imagine some of the scenes before Mark's segment of the story. Jairus is a well-respected religious leader, probably known to many in his Jerusalem neighborhood as a serious yet loyal friend. He is not given to emotional outbursts, yet it is clear to his friends that his beloved daughter's sickness is taking an emotional toll on him. In any case, he swallows his pride enough to approach this somewhat strange figure he's heard about from others. He's desperate; no one seems to know how to help his daughter, so he figures he might as well see what Jesus can do. "Just try!" we hear him saying in front of a group of strangers—anxious, afraid for his daughter, unmindful of his own pride. Jairus is fully a parent in that moment.

Mark rejoins the story after describing an equally audacious woman who wants to touch Jesus' clothes in order to be healed—another desperate person reaching out to him for help. What happens next, though, must have felt to Jairus like a punch in the stomach: some people from his house (servants of this man, meaning he must be well-off) come and tell him that his daughter has died and that he should not trouble the teacher any longer. We can imagine Jairus' contorted face and the shock of grief he must have felt. Was it this reaction that caused Jesus to respond with kind words? "Do not be afraid; just have faith." What was Jairus feeling? Faith in what? A parent's desperation at the loss of a child is unnameable, yet Jesus reassures Jairus that all will yet be well. Mark continues the story:

> When they arrived at the house of the synagogue official, he caught sight of a commotion, people weeping and wailing loudly. So he went in and said to them, "Why this commotion and weeping? The child is not dead but asleep." And they ridiculed him. Then he put them all out. He took along the child's father and mother and those who were with him and entered the room where the child was. He took the child by the hand and said to her, "Talitha koum," which means, "Little girl, I say to you, arise!" The girl, a child of twelve, arose immediately and walked around. (At that) they were utterly astounded. He gave strict orders that no one should know this and said that she should be given something to eat. (Mk 10:38–43)

At Jairus's house, people are already grieving the loss of the child; it is clear from the story that the little girl has been dead for some time. Mark describes the incredulity of the friends when Jesus says she is not dead—they think he's some kind of lunatic. But then, the unthinkable happens: she is raised from the dead.[9] Mark describes them as "astounded" (or "ecstatic" as the Greek word suggests). They can hardly believe their eyes. It would take them some time to digest what has just happened, and so Jesus is clear they should not run off and shout the news to everyone.

Perhaps it is the neighbors of Jairus who keep this experience close to their hearts, wondering who this man is that raised Jairus's daughter back to life. Is he a magician? A prophet of God? Perhaps over time, as they look around at their own lives, they become aware of their own desires for healing. Perhaps he can remove my arthritis! Maybe he can help my son walk again! Maybe he can cure my daughter's blindness! It is no surprise Mark's line in chapter 10 is so straightforward: "people were bringing children to him that he might touch them." Often parents become like Jairus, willing to sacrifice their pride to advocate for their children's needs. Mark describes the disciples as annoyed with this crush of people, but Jesus sees through the parents' pushy behavior to the roots of their desire to care for their children. He says, "Let the children come to me; do not prevent them, for the kingdom of God belongs to such as these." But who are "these"? The Greek text is not clear. Perhaps Jesus was pointing to the parents, whose single-minded devotion to their children was evidence of their total embrace of the vocation to love. Perhaps the line might be rendered, "Let the children come to me; do not prevent [the parents from doing this], for the kingdom of God belongs to [people] such as these [kinds of parents]." On the other hand, perhaps what Jesus meant was the Kingdom of God belongs to children who can elicit from adults wholehearted love and devotion, and the more we welcome children as Jesus did, the more we come to understand and dwell in the Kingdom of God.

Elsewhere, in Matthew's gospel, Jesus praises children and those who care for them:

> The disciples approached Jesus and said, "Who is the greatest in the Kingdom of heaven?" He called a child over, placed it in their midst, and said, "Amen, I say to you, unless you turn and become like children, you will not enter the Kingdom of heaven. Whoever becomes humble like this child is the greatest in the Kingdom of heaven. And whoever receives one child such as this in my name receives me. (18:1–5)

In any case, it is clear Jesus is moved by the scene of parents desiring that he touch their children. We can sympathize with their desire. How often do we reach out to God—in joy, in hope, in fear, in grief, in terror, in longing—that God might make all things well? This is what the parents in Mark's short story are feeling: that Jesus might act like God and make all things well.

At the heart of Christian spirituality is a faith that coming to know the person of Jesus is the way to know God intimately. Jairus and the other people who wanted to speak to Jesus were not unusually religious; they were just parents who cared for their children, so they sought out someone whom they had heard could do good things. Our situation is often no different: we seek Jesus because we hope he can do good things for our children.

These stories point us to two ideas that might help us in cultivating a family spirituality. The first is that like the people pressing upon Jesus, we rely on the witness of others to help us know how to assist our children. The second is that using scriptural texts can help us know Jesus more clearly. We'll look at each of these ideas in turn.

CHAPTER TWELVE

THE WITNESS OF OTHERS

When she was younger, one of our daughters was experiencing problems at her school. She wasn't thriving academically and was facing challenging social dynamics. We started talking to other parents about their children's experiences with the classroom. We talked to teachers and school administrators to get their takes on the situation. What did they see in the social dynamics? How were their children handling the schoolwork? Over time, we began to talk to parents of children in other schools to learn about their experiences. We gained perspective, the ability to see the situation from more than just our own limited views.

Eventually, we decided it was time to switch schools. The decision was a long and difficult one to make because it involved not only our daughter's emotional separation from the environment she'd become accustomed to, but it was also a significant financial commitment on our part. We had to trust in the discernment process that led to the decision and pray it was a good one. Over time, it became clear that it was.

Any consequential decision for our children takes time and becomes clearer to us when we are willing to listen to others' experiences. And while other people's stories cannot determine what's good for our families, still they can help us to understand things from different perspectives. What is clear in the story of Jairus is that he relied on the witness of others enough to humble himself to ask for Jesus' help. Similarly, we relied on the witness of others—specifically, those who were willing to talk about their children's experience at the new school.

Jesus' ministry relied on the witness of many: on the disciples, willing to go out and talk about the Kingdom of God (Lk 10:1–11); on figures like the Samaritan woman, willing to tell her town about Jesus (Jn 4:1–42); on men like Peter (Acts 2:14–36) and Paul (Acts 13:16–41), willing to preach in Jesus' name. The earliest church was a community of witnesses willing to share their stories about how their lives were touched by Jesus. Today, even after two millennia, at its root the Church is similarly a community of witnesses. And like the parents of children at the school our daughter eventually joined, they are people whose experiences can help us understand our own. Perhaps the strongest argument for participating in a church community is sharing the stories of what Jesus has meant for our lives.

Christian spirituality—as distinct from Christian worship as a public act that we do out of habit or out of a desire to be on the same page with other family members—begins when we make personal what is proclaimed by the witness of others. Sue's mother has a saying: "God doesn't have any grandchildren," meaning that at some point in every person's life is the need to make a choice about whether or not to be in relationship with God directly, and not only because of the wishes of a parent. The witness of others is good, but it's not sufficient to sustain us throughout our lives. At some point, we must take the risk to know him, heart to heart. And the only way to do that is through prayer.

Getting started, or continuing, is as simple as using the imagination.

CHAPTER THIRTEEN

READING SCRIPTURE

There is an ancient term for the kind of reading of Bible texts we used earlier in the stories of Jairus and of Jesus with children. *Lectio divina* or "sacred reading" developed in the early centuries of the Church as a way of meditating on the meaning of sacred texts. Lectio divina is to reading what savoring a meal is to eating: it requires slowing down, paying attention, becoming aware of all that the text elicits from us. In a word, it requires imagination. And what makes this ancient practice so wonderful for families is the fact that children are great at imagining, and therefore, they can teach adults a lot about prayer.

At this point, it's important to highlight a key point: we're not talking about how you currently understand the Bible. We're not interested in debates about the relationship between the Bible and the sciences, whether biblical figures were real or fictional, whether the Bible gives clear directions about contentious moral issues today, or whether it predicts the end of time. There is a time and place for those kinds of questions, but this isn't it. We're interested in how biblical texts can be a springboard for prayer and how they invite us into conversation with God in our family vocation—in other words, how they help us to pray and live the rules.

> We're interested in how biblical texts can be a springboard for prayer and how they invite us into conversation with God in our family vocation—in other words, how they help us to pray and live the rules.

So let's be very clear about what we are proposing. First, we'll say something about prayer in general, and then we'll discuss prayer with scripture.

Prayer, in general, is talking with God. If God is God, then we can do this at any time, in any place, under any circumstance. We need neither a church nor a sacred text; we can pray at home, at work, in nature; in peace, in stress, in hope. We can pray alone, with friends or family, or with strangers. God, the Author of Everything, is present in everything the way that an author is present in every word of a book he or she writes. Everything reveals God, and so everything can be a reminder or an opportunity to encounter God. Of course, it is often easier to become mindful of God in the presence of beauty than in the presence of evil or suffering—more on that later. The bottom line is that if God is to be found in all things, then all things can remind us to pray.

Perhaps you are one of those people who feels awkward praying. You're a little self-conscious about being too churchy in church, or you feel as though people are talking to themselves when asked to participate in a public prayer. To be sure, there is a risk in prayer: we open ourselves to feeling foolish. It may be comforting to know, then, that even monks, whose lives are built on a strict regimen of prayer, can encounter a similar doubt—the sense that all these holy words amount to nothing. Prayer is an act of faith, meaning we can't be certain what will happen (if anything) when we do it. But what is clear is that Jesus himself invited people to prayer. Think of the words of the Our Father as a good example or about his counsel to pray in secret and not for the adulation of others (Mt 6:6). Moreover, Christian history testifies to the hundreds of saints and good men and women whose lives were built upon prayer, upon intimacy with God. And the reason is clear: prayer is the way we come to know God as a friend who accompanies us at all times, in joy and hope as well as in pain and suffering.

Scripture is one place where God is to be found, but a privileged place. It's special the way a love letter is special to a beloved. The beloved may have the lover on his or her mind always, especially in the first bloom of love. I think of my beloved when I hear a special song, or when I see the same kind of car he/she drives, or when I pass near where he/she works. But the letter comes directly from the lover, so it is special. So too with scripture: we call it the Word of God.

We understand that phrase "Word of God" today in ways that differ from those of the ancients. Biblical scholars can trace the roots of biblical texts to even more ancient Near Eastern texts; they can point out the literary devices used by the evangelists; they can weigh the historical claims of the many writers of biblical texts against the archaeological and literary evidence. We can trace the development of the biblical canon and see the way later editors used or discarded texts written by earlier writers. In short, we don't see the Word of God in a naïve way, as though God himself took out a pen and started writing. What we do see, however, is God present through the whole process of human beings asking questions, experiencing the ups and downs of a history, praising God in song and poem and myth and story, and collecting and disseminating texts to future generations. To call the Bible the "Word of God" is to suggest that the historical process of this wisdom-passing is fraught with holiness—more than just the collection of a people's wisdom as one might find, say, in the National Archives in Washington, DC. The Bible is a collection that was crafted over a millennium: generations upon generations of people weighing their lives against the words of those gone before, seeking to live meaningfully and lovingly in the face of mystery. For Christians, most importantly, the New Testament collects the astonishing stories and words of Jesus himself, who not only testified to God but who, the writers came to realize, was God himself walking among them, in the flesh. For them, the words were not only those of people reaching out in faith to the object of their longing; the words were those of the object of their longing speaking directly to them. And his words, the words of a divine lover, were sacred.

> The Bible is not only the words of people reaching out in faith to the object of their longing; the words are also those of the object of their longing speaking directly to them.

For this reason, prayer with scripture has special meaning. It is related to the kind of prayer that one makes in nature or alone in the quiet or even in the midst of a busy day because it originates in human desire. What makes scripture theologically different from other words is the belief that the real desires that gave rise to the words originate in God himself, in the inspiration of the Holy Spirit in the lives of the authors. Prayer with scripture involves a kind of receptivity: a listening to words that have developed meaning over time and that can also speak to us immediately. The prophet Isaiah put words to the way that scripture functions as the language of prayer:

> Seek the Lord while he may be found, call him while he is near. Let the scoundrel forsake his way, and the wicked man his thoughts; let him turn to the LORD for mercy; to our God, who is generous in forgiving. For my thoughts are not your thoughts, nor are your ways my ways, says the Lord. As high as the heavens are above the earth, so high are my ways above your ways and my thoughts above your thoughts. For just as from the heavens the rain and snow come down and do not return there till they have watered the earth, making it fertile and fruitful, giving seed to him who sows and bread to him who eats, so shall my word be that goes forth from my mouth; it shall not return to me void, but shall do my will, achieving the end for which I sent it. (Is 55:6–11)

Isaiah imagines the Word of God as nourishing the earth and, in time, nourishing people, whether or not they are thinking about it. Reading and praying with scripture is like taking in spiritual nourishment. The psalmist reflects a similar sentiment:

> As the deer longs for streams of water, so my soul longs for you, O God. My soul thirsts for God, the living God. When can I enter and see the face of God? (Ps 42:2–3)

The poem suggests that the soul naturally reaches out in longing for God, that spiritual hunger is built into us naturally. We've seen this hunger in our children's questions: "Where do we go when we die?" and "Does God have hands?" We all have a spontaneous desire to understand things, especially those things that seem just beyond the grasp of our understanding. Scripture immerses us in a history of those who have taken that hunger seriously and sought to give language to the desires of the heart.

> It's important for us to read scripture as adults in order to help our children learn scripture as children.

All these ruminations about scripture are about a fundamental point: it's important for us to read scripture as adults in order to help our children learn scripture as children. All parents know that it's impossible to preach the lesson "Do as I say, not as I do," especially when it comes to faith and religion. If we want our children to develop compassion for others, reverence for themselves and their gifts, awareness of God's grace in all creation, a sense of purpose and meaning in their lives, a hope amidst times of despair, and a pervading sense that God loves all people, then we must model for them how our own lives are shaped by the imitation of Jesus. In short, we want them to grow into the same sense of conviction that the apostle Peter eventually embraced after walking with Jesus for a while: "Master, to whom shall we go? You have the words of eternal life. We have come to believe and are convinced that you are the Holy One of God" (Jn 6:68).

Participating in public liturgy is a great way to start, for in liturgy we hear the public proclamation of the Christian story. But even better is finding creative ways to share that same story in the home. We propose here four stories, but there are many others you can use throughout the year. We'll approach these stories through a kind of lectio divina appropriate for imitating Jesus as a family through the cultivating of imagination.

CHAPTER FOURTEEN

SEARCHING FOR JESUS

The story of Jesus meeting Zacchaeus is a short one, but it is a helpful entryway to enlivening biblical stories for your children while at the same time deepening your own adult response to Jesus. Here is the story:

> [Jesus] came to Jericho and intended to pass through the town. Now a man there named Zacchaeus, who was a chief tax collector and also a wealthy man, was seeking to see who Jesus was; but he could not see him because of the crowd, for he was short in stature. So he ran ahead and climbed a sycamore tree in order to see Jesus, who was about to pass that way. When he reached the place, Jesus looked up and said to him, "Zacchaeus, come down quickly, for today I must stay at your house." And he came down quickly and received him with joy. When they all saw this, they began to grumble, saying, "He has gone to stay at the house of a sinner." But Zacchaeus stood there and said to the Lord, "Behold, half of my possessions,

Lord, I shall give to the poor, and if I have extorted anything from anyone I shall repay it four times over." And Jesus said to him, "Today salvation has come to this house because this man too is a descendant of Abraham. For the Son of Man has come to seek and to save what was lost." (Lk 19:1–10)

This is a great story to tell to children because it's funny to imagine this short, rich man scrambling up a tree just to get a good look at Jesus. Try to use your own imagination to fill in the gaps of the story you tell your children.

Imagine the story of Zacchaeus with your children. What does Zacchaeus look like? Is he handsome or ugly? How does he act? If he were alive today, what car would he drive? How do you imagine Zacchaeus usually treating people? People call him a sinner—does he deserve it? Is he selfish? Or is he just a good, hardworking man whom people are jealous of? What is he wearing? Does he flaunt his wealth? Would he be wearing an expensive suit today? How does he sound? Does he have a nasally voice or a strong one? What does the air feel like? The bark of the sycamore tree? The fine clothes of Zacchaeus? The scratchy cloth worn by the poorer residents of the town? Why does he climb the tree? Is he just doing celebrity-watching, or are his motives pure? What does he look like when he's up there? What is Jesus' reaction? Does Jesus stifle a laugh? Why does Jesus choose Zacchaeus of all the people around him? What is it about Zacchaeus that catches Jesus' attention? Why doesn't Jesus choose someone more humble?

Luke sets up the story to put emphasis on Jesus' closing line: "Today salvation has come to this house because this man too is a descendant of Abraham. For the Son of Man has come to seek and to save what was lost." Tax collectors, who collaborated with the despised Roman occupiers of the region, were seen as traitors. What sets Zacchaeus apart, though, is a desire to see Jesus, to learn about him. Luke wants to show that Jesus has come even for such people, to incite in them a desire for something more than the kind of happiness that wealth and power can bring.

What does such an image elicit in you? Does the idea that Jesus wants to save the "lost" (in this case, those seduced by wealth and power)—to bring them closer to God—have meaning for you? To put it more starkly, what does faith in Jesus save you from?

> Our freedom of choice is limited by a small understanding of what is ultimately good for us.

Consider these same questions from the perspective of your children. How might it make a difference to them to look at the world the way Jesus does in this story? Does teaching them to imitate Jesus offer them a unique way of looking at the world? What might Jesus save them from?

Let's be clear about what we're suggesting here. Children are not usually notorious sinners in dire need of repentance. We're not talking about children in the "I once was lost but now am found, was blind but now I see" kind of way. But we are suggesting that kids can develop stubborn habits based on getting what they want, and sometimes those habits (and the things they want) are bad for them. In our family, there are rather constant battles over things like TV, junk food, computer games, iPod use, and so on. If left to their own devices, our kids would quickly develop some pretty horrible habits. Saint Paul pointed to a fundamental problem that all people face, kids included: sometimes we do things we know we shouldn't because our freedom of choice is limited by a small and sadly somewhat self-centered understanding of what is ultimately good for us.

What makes the story of Zacchaeus interesting, then, is the fact that this small, rich man had what most adults consider a pretty decent lifestyle, yet he did something extraordinary: he sought out a preacher who was talking about being blessed by God in poverty, humility, and the practice of justice (see the Beatitudes on page 56). In other words, he was willing to see past his small desires to wonder what Jesus was really all about.

So, back to the question: What might Jesus save our children from? Perhaps being trapped by their small desires. Remember that Zacchaeus was not particularly well liked. Remember that others around Zacchaeus grumbled when Jesus called him down, and they referred to Zacchaeus as a sinner. (We imagine it like the way a conservative today might call someone a liberal, or vice versa: "He's not one of us. He's wrong about everything.") Ask your child sometime whether he or she knows someone whom others regard that way, and ask your son or daughter what it might be like to be as welcoming to that child as Jesus was to Zacchaeus. Remind your child to reach out to other children who feel isolated as Zacchaeus was.

If you are a churchgoer with your children, this next example may be helpful. Consider the ways that over the course of the year, the whole Church seeks to draw the faithful into encounters with Jesus. Think about a Christmas pageant, where we are drawn into the story of the Nativity, or a Palm Sunday procession, when we are on the streets of Jerusalem for Jesus' triumphal entry. The point of these practices is to cultivate a religious imagination, an intimacy with Jesus through participation in the story of his life. Give your child, then, the chance to be like Zacchaeus, to run after Jesus in the hope of meeting him firsthand, so to speak. How? By giving him or her chances to imagine Jesus directly. Allow your child to stand on the pew during the consecration of the Eucharist, pretending to be Zacchaeus in the tree, gazing over the heads of fellow parishioners. Or take a moment to go to the tabernacle after Mass and talk to your child about Jesus' presence in the Eucharist. Cultivate in your child's imagination the kind of desire to see Jesus that Zacchaeus showed.

The point of cultivating imagination in a biblical story is that it allows both adults and children to encounter the story in more than an abstract way, to ask, along with the words of the beautiful hymn, "Were you there?" There's a theological truth hidden underneath this practice, namely that God is always and everywhere trying to get our attention and turn our attention to greater love, greater life, greater hope, greater faith. Just as an ordinary story can make you look at the world in a new way, so too can a gospel story make you look at Jesus in a new way. The Church's word for that experience is "conversion."

CHAPTER FIFTEEN

CONVERSION AND FORGIVENESS

Perhaps the most famous story of conversion is the one commonly known as the Prodigal Son. We prefer to call it the story of the Lost Son primarily because most people have no idea what the word "prodigal" means. (It means wasteful.) The story focuses on two main characters and a third minor character whose reaction is also important to the story. Ultimately, it is a story about forgiveness.

> A man had two sons, and the younger son said to his father, "Father, give me the share of your estate that should come to me." So the father divided the property between them. After a few days, the younger son collected all his belongings and set off to a distant country where he squandered his inheritance on a life of dissipation. When he had freely spent everything, a severe famine struck that country, and he found himself in dire need. So he hired himself out to one of the local citizens who sent him to his farm to tend the swine. And he longed to eat his fill of the pods on which the swine fed, but nobody gave

him any. Coming to his senses he thought, "How many of my father's hired workers have more than enough food to eat, but here am I, dying from hunger. I shall get up and go to my father and I shall say to him, 'Father, I have sinned against heaven and against you. I no longer deserve to be called your son; treat me as you would treat one of your hired workers." So he got up and went back to his father. While he was still a long way off, his father caught sight of him, and was filled with compassion. He ran to his son, embraced him and kissed him. His son said to him, "Father, I have sinned against heaven and against you; I no longer deserve to be called your son." But his father ordered his servants, "Quickly bring the finest robe and put it on him; put a ring on his finger and sandals on his feet. Take the fattened calf and slaughter it. Then let us celebrate with a feast, because this son of mine was dead, and has come to life again; he was lost, and has been found." Then the celebration began. Now the older son had been out in the field and, on his way back, as he neared the house, he heard the sound of music and dancing. He called one of the servants and asked what this might mean. The servant said to him, "Your brother has returned and your father has slaughtered the fattened calf because he has him back safe and sound." He became angry, and when he refused to enter the house, his father came out and pleaded with him. He said to his father in reply, "Look, all these years I served you and not once did I disobey your orders; yet you never gave me even a young goat to feast on with my friends. But when your son returns who swallowed up your property with prostitutes, for him you slaughter the fattened calf." He said to him, "My son, you are here with me always; everything I have is yours. But now we must celebrate and rejoice, because your brother was dead and has come to life again; he was lost and has been found." (Lk 15:11–32)

On the surface, this is a story about a father forgiving his son. As such, it's a good reminder to parents and children alike that, as Christians, we are called to practice this kind of love in the family, even when it is not easy. But this is also a story about sibling rivalry and jealousy as well as filial obedience and disobedience. It's about choosing a diminished kind of freedom over family love and coming to one's senses about the importance of preserving family ties, even though that realization may initially come from a selfish place (the son only comes to his senses because he is humiliated and starving and remembers that conditions at home are better, even for the lowest servants).

Another way to understand this story is to see it as one about growing up. It's not too hard to imagine the lost son as a college student heading off on his own, partying and avoiding adult responsibility to the point of squandering his resources. In an age when more and more young adults are living with their parents well into their twenties and thirties and when there are so many cultural messages about staying young and carefree (and irresponsible), this story can focus our attention on the need to come to an adult understanding of the importance of family. The moment of the lost son's conversion is when he compares the misery he's gotten himself into with the generosity of his father, and he chooses to let go of his autonomy to be back home.

Many adults today can identify with the sense of unrest they felt as an adolescent at home, wishing to have more freedom from parental rules. If you have teens or preteens at home, perhaps you sense this same unrest in them. Perhaps at times you have even felt that your life could be easier if they moved away. What's remarkable about the story, and what Jesus' original listeners would have observed immediately, is the fact that the father acts in an unseemly way upon hearing of his son's return. One can, without too much trouble, imagine that before the son's departure, he was a bit of a spoiled young man, likely manipulating his father and irritating his brother. More importantly, his request for an early inheritance would have seemed like a slap in his father's face, effectively saying to him, "I wish you were dead now, so I can have my money." So the fact that the father acts as he does upon the son's return is striking—even foolish. Suggesting, as Jesus did, that God the Father's love is like that of the father in the story would have appeared ludicrous to his hearers—weak, shameful, irresponsible, even scandalous. Yet from other parables that Jesus uses to describe the Father, like that of the widow who searches for the lost coin (Lk 15:8–10) and the good shepherd who goes after the lost sheep (Lk 15:3–7 and Mt 18:12–14), it is clear that Jesus is very deliberate in making exactly that connection. God will go to absurd ends to show his love for us.

> God will go to absurd ends to show his love for us.
> We should do the same for our children.

Sharing this story with children of any age is an opportunity to emphasize how permanent our love for them is. When one of our daughters was little, having come home shortly after we adopted her, she had an insatiable need for the kind of deep personal attention she was unable to receive in the orphanage. We had to be in physical contact with her literally twenty-four hours a day, or she would get panicked. Often she would drag Sue across the room just to pick up a toy. And yet even with this inordinate demand for attention, both of us were happy to oblige in the belief that somehow we were healing the loss she'd experienced as an infant.

> Love is not an answer to the question, "How do you feel?" but rather, "What are you willing to do?"

Many parents can immediately identify with going to absurd ends to show their love for their children. To come at this truth from another angle, let's pay attention to the fact that parenthood summons from us acts of love that we could never have imagined or planned but that can often surprise us with their power. In our experience, there is simply no more profound evidence of God in our lives than the simple fact that we have experienced powerful expressions of love. They have challenged us to see love as much more than an answer to the question, "How do you feel?" Rather, they have enabled us to see love as an answer to the question, "What are you willing to do?"

The father in the story may very well have felt wounded by the lost son, perhaps even confiding in the older son how grieved he was by the younger's cruelty. Perhaps the older son played the role of his father's comforter for many years, sharing his father's burden and developing a deep resentment of his younger brother's selfishness. Could it be that even earlier that day the father shared with his son his grief, only to see the young son come back to life, as it were, by his return? Could the older son have seen through the younger's charade, scared that his return would only offer him a renewed opportunity to break his father's heart?

And yet, at the center of the story, there is the father running in a most undignified way out to meet the younger son. Can you identify with that experience of doing something humiliating for the sake of a child? Can you recall the thoughts going through your head, along the lines of "she really needs to learn a lesson here" or "he's really going to get it for this one" even as you seize the opportunity to show compassion, forgiveness, love? Parenting can offer us—sometimes daily—a whole range of emotions, but so very often the emotions have to take a backseat to a more basic question of what we choose to do and how we choose to show our children we love them, sometimes in spite of what we are actually feeling.

> Practicing how to forgive instills the habit of separating the emotions of the moment from the work of building loving relationships.

Children, especially young ones, live in a world governed by their feelings. What they feel is what they do. When they get hurt, they want to hurt back so that things are fair. The story of the Lost Son offers a chance to look at life a little differently, to imagine the importance of moving beyond how you feel to consider what good family relationships require. When Jesus told this story to the Pharisees, he was suggesting that the obedient sons of the law—the older sons of the world—were jealous of those younger sons whom God embraced with forgiveness. He was suggesting that it was important to let go of jealousy toward those who had sinned and repented, only to be welcomed back by God. Children (and adults, for that matter) can feel similar jealousy toward those who "get away with it," who act selfishly but then are forgiven. It is natural to desire fairness, but the parable suggests that what is even more important than fairness is a willingness to forgive—"seventy times seven times," Jesus says elsewhere (Mt 18:21–22).

Parents can appreciate this lesson in a way that children can only learn later. Cultivating forgiveness in the home is necessary for a family's life lest it descend into constant competition and deception. While it is also necessary to cultivate a sense of justice so that there isn't an escalation of seeing what kids can get away with, practicing how to forgive instills the habit of separating the emotions of the moment from the work of building loving relationships. Parents can model lessons, such as saying, "I'm angry that you did this, but I love you and want to move on." We can also give children the opportunity to say how they feel about a sibling's misdeed while encouraging them to forgive the other and go on with a game or activity. The focus in the story, and the focus in a family's life, is on repairing the relationships even to the point of being excessive—a "prodigal"—with one's compassion.

PRACTICING FORGIVENESS

Parents can teach their children how to practice forgiveness every time there is a squabble. Learn what your child needs when he or she is angry: Is it counting to ten? Is it taking time alone in a room before rejoining a playmate? Whatever it is, allow the child to learn that coping mechanism and then speak words of forgiveness to the other child. "It's OK. I forgive you." Tell them that practicing forgiveness is like learning to let go of the "banana" called anger (see page 62).

CHAPTER SIXTEEN

COMPASSION

Compassion is at the heart of the gospel as much as at the heart of an authentic family life. The word "compassion" comes from Latin, meaning "suffering with," and points us to the central mystery of Jesus' life: the fact that he was God living among us in the flesh, not conquering the world but rather sharing in our suffering.

The most poignant story of compassion in the New Testament is perhaps the most well known of Jesus' parables, that of the Good Samaritan. Indeed, today the word "Samaritan" (which in Jesus' time was just the name of the Israelites who lived in what had been the northern kingdom of Samaria) has become synonymous with "compassionate." The story is a kind of moral catechism, illustrating the challenge and the beauty of living compassionately. A lawyer asks Jesus about what it meant to be a neighbor in God's eyes, and Jesus responds with this story.

> A man fell victim to robbers as he went down from Jerusalem to Jericho. They stripped and beat him and went off leaving him half-dead. A priest happened to be going down that road, but when he saw

him, he passed by on the opposite side. Likewise a
Levite came to the place, and when he saw him, he
passed by on the opposite side. But a Samaritan traveler who came upon him was moved with compassion at the sight. He approached the victim, poured
oil and wine over his wounds and bandaged them.
Then he lifted him up on his own animal, took him
to an inn and cared for him. The next day he took
out two silver coins and gave them to the innkeeper
with the instruction, "Take care of him. If you spend
more than what I have given you, I shall repay you
on my way back." (Lk 10:30–35)

Like many of Jesus' parables, this story appeals immediately to
the imagination: one can see the road, the travelers, the disgust or
unease of those who passed by, the look of concern on the Samaritan's face. This imaginative dimension also makes the story easy to
adapt to any time or place to help children understand the basic idea.

Jesus is devastatingly straightforward in the story, ingeniously
presenting the passersby as people who could claim they had their
reasons for avoiding the victim but who clearly should have known
and done better. They are religious leaders trained in God's law but
who, it seems, have lost the forest for the trees. They strive to obey
ritual laws but forget that all of the laws are in service to the more
expansive good of God's care for his people. This story, like others
in which Jesus seeks to reorient people's understanding of religious
law,[10] was about calling people to understand the Kingdom of God
as a place where compassionate love spilled over all existing boundaries of human experience like water over a dam. Compassion in
the Kingdom was about generosity beyond what is reasonable, tres-
passing boundaries of propriety, going the extra mile in heroic love.

Compassion   103

The Samaritan, a member of a northern people despised by the southerners, was the one who didn't care about how much caring for the victim cost. He didn't just run to get help, or assume that someone else would take care of the problem. He poured a huge amount of time and money into assuring the victim that he would be well.

Remember that rule four is that God calls us to build his Kingdom of beauty, truth, justice, and mercy through our love for one another. The story of the Good Samaritan is an illustration of that call and of a person who was willing to build the Kingdom by performing a selfless act. What makes the story striking for us today is that, if we are honest with ourselves, we can identify with those who pass victims by because they are hurrying on their way to "something important." How many times have we seen someone on the side of the road, assuming that he or she must have a cell phone to call for help? How often have we been in a rush to get somewhere and remained oblivious to other people? We live in a fast-paced world and can often fail to see others in need.

> Pay attention to the desires that motivate your daily habits. Help your children learn to ask what desires motivate their choices, too.

The parable is challenging because it calls us to pay attention to the desires that motivate our daily habits. It's easy to fall into cruise control, going through the usual motions of the day without much thought to others. The priest and the Levite in the story are not bad men; they are simply seeing the world in a smaller way than the Samaritan does. The Samaritan appears as a person on the lookout for opportunities to express love in action, to build the Kingdom in whatever ways might present themselves. He is portrayed as some-one not fundamentally concerned with himself but rather with the role he might play in the unfolding of the Kingdom. Elsewhere Jesus makes the somewhat obscure remark that whoever holds on to his life will lose it but that the one who loses his life for the sake of the Kingdom will find it (see Jn 12:25, Lk 17:33, Mt 10:39). In light of this parable, it's a little easier to understand what he means: letting go of selfishness and living for something greater than ourselves can give our lives purpose and meaning, satisfying more deeply rooted desires than the ones we pay attention to when we stroke our own egos.

Family life is a crucible of letting go of our egos. It is critical that parents model for children what it means to live compassion-ately, to practice obvious acts that show children how to choose to participate in building a Kingdom larger than oneself. Maybe it will involve babysitting friends' children so that those friends can have time off or go out on a date. Maybe it will mean volunteer-ing at school or coaching a team. Maybe it will involve giving up a weekend to go camping with the scouting troop. Whatever the action, we continuously have opportunities to connect our choices with those of the Good Samaritan. By introducing the story to our children, we have a good image to return to when we are asking them to give up what they want for something greater, such as inviting the new kid at school for a playdate or walking the elderly neighbor's dog. There are a host of ways each day that we can begin to train our children to look for opportunities to act for the King-dom the way the Good Samaritan did.

IMITATING THE GOOD SAMARITAN

Spend a few minutes over dinner asking your children whom they'd like to pray for. Who did they see in need over the course of their day? Do any kids at school need help? Are there people in the neighborhood who are sick, grieving, or stressed? Get in the habit of asking your children to be aware of others' needs, so that they can cultivate the habit of being on the lookout for how they might be a voice of comfort to others. Teach them to seek out the lonely child on the playground or invite the new kid for a playdate.

CHAPTER SEVENTEEN

FAMILY CELEBRATION

According to John's gospel, the very first miracle Jesus performed was at a wedding in a town not far from where he grew up, called Cana. It's a remarkable story of his mother, Mary, feeling sad for the wedding party and urging a still-not-totally-ready-for-the-public-eye Jesus to do something wonderful to help them out. Her urging is not on behalf of a desperate widow trying to feed her family or for a blind man or leper wanting to be healed, nor is it a plea for world peace or freedom from the Roman army occupying their homeland. Instead, it's a prompting to get the wedding party more wine.

> On the third day there was a wedding in Cana in Galilee, and the mother of Jesus was there. Jesus and his disciples were also invited to the wedding. When the wine ran short, the mother of Jesus said to him, "They have no wine." Jesus said to her, "Woman, how does your concern affect me? My hour has not yet come." His mother said to the servers, "Do whatever he tells you." Now there were six stone water jars

there for Jewish ceremonial washings, each holding twenty to thirty gallons. Jesus told them, "Fill the jars with water." So they filled them to the brim. Then he told them, "Draw some out now and take it to the headwaiter." So they took it. And when the headwaiter tasted the water that had become wine, without knowing where it came from (although the servers who had drawn the water knew), the headwaiter called the bridegroom and said to him, "Everyone serves good wine first, and then when people have drunk freely, an inferior one; but you have kept the good wine until now." (Jn 2:1–10)

The story does not involve the scared teenage single mother we first encountered at the story of the Annunciation, in which the angel told her she would bear a son named Jesus. Here, Mary is a canny, mature woman who won't take "no" as an answer from her son. She sees an opportunity for him to do some good, and she puts him up to it. It's funny to imagine Jesus in a position similar to our children when they don't want to do that thing we've signed them up for (soccer, camp, music lessons, whatever). Mary's implicit answer is very much like our own: You're going to do it whether you like it or not. I'm your mother! (Notice her restraint, too, at Jesus' somewhat smart response to her, calling her "woman." Indeed!)

Mary's wisdom is in recognizing that this comparatively minor mishap—not ordering enough wine—is casting a shadow on what should be an occasion for rejoicing. We can imagine the scene: the bridegroom is sweating as he sees more and more guests show up, tallying in his mind how much people drink and how much wine he's actually ordered. Unlike many of the other guests, Mary sees the problem. Perhaps she discerns the look of discomfort on the bridegroom's face. Perhaps she sees the way that the waitstaff are refilling cups only halfway, to stretch the remaining amount of wine. Perhaps she sees the headwaiter going to the bridegroom, whispering something as he wipes his forehead, looking stressed.

Resolved, she decides this is the time for a *mitzvah*, a righteous deed in obedience to God's law. She knows who Jesus is and what he can do, having (no doubt) helped him to understand his gifts during childhood and adolescence. She is fully aware that doing such a *mitzvah* in a public place will get people talking about him. But she feels for the couple and the family, and she understands that a wedding is a moment of rejoicing that must not be cut short. Perhaps she had in mind the lines from one of the holy books, the Song of Songs:

> Daughters of Jerusalem, come forth
> and look upon King Solomon
> In the crown with which his mother has crowned him
> on the day of his marriage,
> on the day of the joy of his heart. (3:11)

Perhaps she says to herself that God is exalted in the joy of people's hearts, and this celebration of a marriage also gives joy to the heart of God.

In any case, she urges Jesus to perform a miracle, and he does, almost without thinking. But perhaps Jesus himself learns something on that day after the bridegroom's face changes from stress to rejoicing, freed from the burden of fear. For later in Jesus' teaching, he will return to the image of the wedding banquet, suggesting that his disciples are like the guests of the bridegroom: "Can the wedding guests fast while the bridegroom is with them? As long as they have the bridegroom with them they cannot fast" (Mk 2:19; see also Mt 9:15 and Lk 5:34). And in the book of the prophet Isaiah, the Lord had described salvation as a feast of rich food and choice wines (25:6), so it is no surprise that Jesus would use this image of a wedding banquet to describe the Kingdom of God:

> The kingdom of heaven may be likened to a king who gave a wedding feast for his son. He dispatched his servants to summon the invited guests to the feast, but they refused to come. A second time he sent other servants, saying, "Tell those invited: 'Behold, I have prepared my banquet, my calves and fattened cattle are killed, and everything is ready; come to the feast.'" (Mt 22:2–4)

The wedding is a family celebration, a remembrance of the past and a hopeful look toward the future. In Jesus' world, a wedding was also a celebration of God's creation of man and woman for each other, of "two in one flesh" who together carried forward God's promise to Abraham to build a great and holy nation. Jesus' first miracle in this context suggests the centrality of the family in God's plan of salvation, as if to suggest that it is enough to build the Kingdom by simply starting with one great family celebration.

It is enough to build the Kingdom by simply starting with one great family celebration.

Today, it is difficult for many families to come together to celebrate. Geographic distance, family arguments, divorce or estrangement, busy schedules, life events, and many other factors can get in the way. But what is suggestive in the story of the wedding at Cana is the fact that it is this rather ordinary context in which the announcement of the Kingdom of God in Jesus' ministry begins. Perhaps our families may not be perfect. (But who's to say that the family at Cana was perfect anyway?) A family celebration is where Jesus comes to begin the announcement of the Kingdom. It is the place where the gladness of all must not be cut short, where there is time for rejoicing, and where the rejoicing will be a sign of the heavenly banquet that God is preparing in our midst.

For our family, Christmas is the season every year that most feels like a doorstep to heaven. Our memories are rich and deep, originating in the stories that we carried from our childhood families. It is a deeply sensory experience: There are the smells of baked goods whose recipes the women in the family have shared for decades. There are the bright lights, trees and wreaths, stockings and gifts. There are Christmas songs and shows and movies. There is the taste of the turkey and ham and potatoes and cranberries and stuffing. There is the feeling of a warm fire, of nestling with one another while sipping tea. These sensory experiences, extended over many days, are like stepping outside of the normal flow of time for a while and resting somewhere in the middle of memories that span generations. We are present for a time with loved ones near and far, alive and dead, and our hearts grow large. It feels like a foretaste of heaven.

What the story of the wedding at Cana suggests to us is that such foretastes are real, and they point us to the desires of our hearts that find fruition in the Kingdom. The family celebrations that we share are important for helping us to know and name those desires, so much deeper and more lasting than the hundred more distracting desires we experience daily. They are important for both adults and children. For adults, these celebrations recall the experiences that pointed them toward their deepest desires. For children, they help teach which desires are more deeply rooted and more authentic. At Cana, Jesus seems to say, "Let the celebration continue! Let not the gladness of the guests be cut short!"—and he says the same to us when we celebrate together. The lesson of Cana is perhaps the one many would find most disarming: that we learn how to build the Kingdom when we party together.

THE FAMILY BANQUET

Rule two is that our family's purpose is to love one another and, through that love, to find joy. Help your children practice this rule at meal time by asking the question, "How can you help the family have a good meal?" Small children can help set the table; older children can help cook. Encourage your children's creativity by asking them to make placemats or a table centerpiece. As they get older, invite your kids to plan meals, do shopping, or take on the task of preparing a meal while the other family members play a game together.

We've shared reflections on these four stories as ways of encouraging you to bring reflection on scripture into interactions with your children. Of course, there are hundreds of stories you can use. One reason why we go to church is to learn these stories over and over, so that they become part of us. There is an ancient sense about stories that we miss in the digital age: that one learns stories not by a quick hyperlink-click-and-glance but by multiple forms of encounter with the story, through sound and action, through song and ritual prayer. Liturgy is a multisensory experience precisely because it aims to make us participants in the very stories we read. Good teachers know this: you can't just read to children or ask them to read things; you must get them to encounter stories through various means.

We encourage you to not only read biblical stories but also to encounter them through the Church's liturgy. Many churches have children's liturgies so that kids can encounter the stories in age-appropriate ways, but even if they don't, you can facilitate that encounter at home. Learn and use scripture in your lessons to them; model the stories and help them make connections. There are as many ways as there are stories. Get a good children's Bible for young children; get a teen or study Bible for older kids. Help them to understand the stories as resources for how to live the rules.

CHAPTER EIGHTEEN

DISCERNMENT AND VOCATION

Ultimately, the rules are about living together well. This means making good choices. Our hope as parents is that our children will imitate our best selves and learn how to make good choices for themselves.

Not long ago, Tim lost a golden opportunity for this kind of lesson. He had taken one of our daughters out to buy basketball shoes at the local sports store. He was enjoying this rare moment one-on-one with our daughter immensely, but just as they were pulling into the parking space, she floored him the way our kids sometimes will. Out of nowhere she asked him point-blank, "Have you ever cheated on Mom?"

Tim had a visceral reaction—"No! Of course not! Why on earth would you even ask that?" He felt defensive, wondering why this sensitive topic should even have come up. Had he said something untoward at some point? What could possibly have given her this idea? Fortunately, she did not probe further, and they continued shopping.

Later, when we talked about the experience, Sue suggested that we use the incident to explain exactly why Tim would never make that kind of choice. Our daughter had likely encountered some story—perhaps in a song lyric or a film—in which someone cheated on someone. Our daughter's question may very likely have been an attempt to learn her dad's perspective on why this can happen and perhaps even to obtain reassurance that he would not make a similar choice. Had Tim not been defensive, he might have been able to draw a straight line between vocation and decision: "I love your mom, so I would never make that kind of unfair choice." Perhaps that kind of explanation would have elicited even more questions about what it means to love someone.

In any family, there is an imperative to learn how to love and how to make decisions that reflect love. As parents, we understand on some basic level that our vocations involve many decisions on a daily basis. In our better moments, we are able to make decisions that aim at some good. We teach our children to eat their vegetables, read good books, get exercise, do well in school, brush their teeth, clean up after themselves, and so on. We try to instill good habits and help them open up their worlds beyond their limited desires for candy or entertainment. But if we're honest with ourselves, we have to admit that often we are too stressed or busy or tired to teach those lessons. We want our kids to make good choices, but we often just have to let them get what they want in a given moment. For that reason, it's important to develop what has been common knowledge among ethicists from at least the time of Aristotle, namely that wise choices are frequently the result not of clever thinking at the moment but of carefully cultivated habits.

Parents know this on a gut level. Anyone who watches young children behave knows they need some measure of structure in their lives. Whether it's something as simple as a bedtime routine or something more complex like polite interaction with adults, all children need regular coaching and practice on how to make choices. What we do is "culture" our children—that is, train them in how to become full participants in the world they inhabit. We don't want them to get stuck in patterns of selfishness or compulsion; rather, we encourage them to grow mindful of others so that they can reap the benefits of relationships and, ultimately, live life to the full.

But what is the culture we want them to inhabit? What is the vision that directs our own choices for our children? This is a practical question. Of all the hours in a week, how many do we want dedicated to school, sports, music, playing with friends, playing on the com-

> [Jesus said,]
> "I came so that they might have life and have it more abundantly."
>
> JOHN 10:10

puter, learning to draw, learning a new language, making crafts, praying and participating in worship, reading for pleasure, and so on? What, in other words, will help us decide what's good for them? What habits will we hope to instill in them? What makes these questions harder, of course, is that as parents, we have to be on the lookout for what their true interests and talents are—we can't automatically assume they will be the same as our own. Children are eager to please their parents, and the pleasure they derive from seeing approval of their efforts can take them a long way in developing their potential. Yet that same desire to please their parents may in the long run hamper children from exploring new talents and interests. We want to culture them, but we also want them to discover what they love and are good at.

Living the rules by making wise decisions is known as *discernment*. Up to this point, we've used the words "discern" and "discernment" in the usual sense of making a choice among many options. From here on, though, we'll use it in the more specific sense that has emerged in the Christian spiritual tradition, primarily in the tradition of Ignatian spirituality. An important point to underscore here is that discernment is really a practice—

> ## Living toward what is good and beautiful and holy is more important than seeking what is most immediately going to make us feel good.

that is, something we do over and over to gain competence, just like practicing piano or shooting baskets—and we want to cultivate this practice of discernment in our children precisely so that they develop the skill of making wise life choices.

Living a Christian life is about going where Jesus points us, even in times of frustration and doubt, mindful that our ability to see the good that comes from that kind of intimacy with Jesus may be limited at a given moment. To say it a bit differently, spirituality is not only about what we feel; it's also about the sober choices we make when life is hard.

What we parents want to pass along to our children, perhaps more than anything else, is the sense that living toward what is good and beautiful and holy is more important than seeking what is most immediately going to make us feel good. We want them to have the sense that there is more to life than a movement from one good feeling to another—that our lives take on great meaning, in fact, when we are willing to take on the sometimes difficult work of building the Kingdom. The prophet Jeremiah gave voice to this call:

I know well the plans I have in mind for you, says
the Lord, plans for your welfare, not for woe! Plans
to give you a future full of hope. (29:11)

Jeremiah wrote these words about God's plans for Israel in the midst of their worst moment in history, a tragic exile from their homeland. As Christians, we believe that God says the same words to each of us, both in good times and bad: God calls each person into being so that each person can play a part within a still-unfolding divine symphony. Our life choices, then, are about discerning that call and, with the help of God's grace, growing into people who are capable of bringing forth music. Our role as parents is to help our children discern the vocation, the life purpose, with which God has endowed them. In so doing, we engage in our own ongoing discernment process, learning more about who we are through the eyes of our children.

In contrast to so many cultural messages that aim to incite personal desires as an engine for consuming things, Christian discernment of desire always involves balancing personal desire with the desires of those whom we are called to love. "Who is my neighbor?" That was the question that prompted Jesus to tell the parable of the Good Samaritan. As we explored earlier, Jesus is suggesting to us that our desires and our happiness ought always to be mindful of the imperative to love others. Jesus' own life and ministry testify to this outward-directed desire: he seemed remarkably unconcerned with himself (how he looked, what he was going to eat, which artists were on his playlist), but he was hyperaware of those around him and how he might bring healing and comfort to those in need.

Jesus' spiritual freedom was rooted in a clear vision of how much of what we think is important is, in the face of eternity, really just a passing fancy. Jesus' attitude reflects the powerful words of the beginning of the book of Ecclesiastes:

> Vanity of vanities, says Qoheleth, vanity of vanities!
> All things are vanity! What profit has man from all
> the labor which he toils at under the sun? (1:2–3)

The author of Ecclesiastes, Qoheleth, observes that so much of life is spent running around, with little meaning in any of it. Pursuing riches and pleasures and power is ultimately fruitless. Thinking about this idea, we have in mind the kind of running around we do each day: Who will pick up the kids from school? Who will drive them to basketball, take them for the playdate, or run over to the PTO meeting? We're so busy—what's it all for? Is teaching them to be busy and competitive the most important lesson about life we want them to absorb?

The only reward, Qoheleth writes, comes from observing God's commands.

> The last word, when all is heard: Fear God and keep
> his commandments, for this is man's all; because God
> will bring to judgment every work, with all its hid-
> den qualities, whether good or bad. (Eccl 12:13–14)

In reflecting the language of Ecclesiastes, Jesus calls us to a similar spiritual freedom. Happiness, he says, is not to be found by looking around at other people and wanting what they have.

> I tell you, do not worry about your life, what you
> will eat (or drink), or about your body, what you
> will wear. Is not life more than food and the body
> more than clothing? Look at the birds in the sky;
> they do not sow or reap, they gather nothing into

barns, yet your heavenly Father feeds them. Are not
you more important than they? (Mt 6:25–26)

Jesus reminds us that a life well lived is a life in which one
becomes adept at discerning which desires are most real, most
life-giving, most rooted in love, most opening of our freedom, and
therefore worth pursuing in making life choices. By contrast, he
invites us to let go of those desires that keep us trapped in patterns
of worry.

For parents, this is good news. Our vocation is to encourage our
children to grow into the people God has created them to be, to
aid them in their own processes of discernment by helping unmask
their false desires. We want to help them grow in self-knowledge
and a vision of the good. Cultivating these habits in our children
is the first step toward helping them develop an active spiritual life
and a foundation for making good choices.

CHAPTER NINETEEN

SELF-KNOWLEDGE AND THE GOOD

When our daughters were still toddlers, we began conversations about what sorts of activities we wanted to expose them to. What, we asked, was important for them to learn? We faced a cascade of choices: Should we prioritize their learning Chinese so that they could one day visit China and see where they are from? What about sports? What about music, art, or something else? As we looked around at other families with small children, we saw a dizzying array of activities (and an equally dizzying level of prices for many of them!). Because we were on a tight budget, some of the choices were easy to eliminate. But we continued to look for opportunities, especially affordable ones. We formed a group of other adoptive parents with Chinese children and learned some rudimentary songs and games in Chinese. We took our girls to culture fairs and on hikes and bike rides as well as the occasional overnight trip to visit friends or family. We read to them, brought them to church, and enrolled them in play groups. Overall, we thought about ways to expose them to many different kinds of activities in order to

> Parents are
> on the lookout for
> what sparks their
> children's interest,
> what gives them energy,
> what makes them want
> to try hard at something.

learn where their talents and interests lie.

In retrospect, what has become clear to us is that in all these choices we were practicing a kind of unselfconscious discernment for our children. Especially as adoptive parents who could not assume that our children would be like we were as children, we were trying to elicit clues about what kind of people God made them to be. Even today, when they are older, we are on the lookout for what sparks their interest, what gives them energy, what makes them want to try hard at something.

Some important lessons we can share with our children are the stories from our past. We can share with them our own struggles to make sense of our lives, to make important life choices, to wrestle with decisions that had long-term impacts on who we are. What Tim regretted about our daughter's question at the sports store was the missed opportunity to tell the story about why he chose to marry Sue and the different choices he might have made instead. We hope to look for other opportunities to tell that story, though, because it is a story we hope might inform the kinds of decisions she makes about relationships in her life.

We want our children to learn what it means to love and be loved so that they will develop habits of discerning true friends. But we also want them to learn how the gifts that God has given them might be put to use in building a good world and how they might use their talents in service to others and thereby find joy. Good grades are fine; talents in music or writing or public speaking or sports or acting or anything else are great; getting a good job or a new house or a car can be lovely. But unless these things are imbued with meaning, the shine will wear off. Our accomplishments have meaning when they are oriented toward the building of the Kingdom—when we have a deep sense that God has blessed us in doing these things because they contribute to the world he is trying to build in love.

Think back to when you were in high school and try to remember what things excited you then. What did you really, really want? What did you spend your time thinking about, hoping for? Now ask yourself: Do you still want those things? Was the A on that test really important, or the attention of that someone for whom you pined? Remember that kids live in a world circumscribed by their limited experience, and what they desire at any given moment is likely to appear to be everything to them. Part of our task is to remind them there is a much larger Good than they can currently understand and to call them to work toward that Good even when it's not clear to them.

> We draw our children into learning experiences that they themselves might not choose but that grant them opportunities to develop self-knowledge and a vision of the Good.

Not long ago, we were helping one of our daughters prepare a project for a science fair. It was a daunting task, bound to be massively time-consuming. To make matters worse, it came during a beautiful fall weekend when all of us would have preferred to be doing something else. But wanting to make sure our daughter followed through with her schoolwork, we plunged in.

We purchased a kit online that provided all the materials for the project and spent the first part of the day putting it all together.

In a little while, our dining room was transformed into a chemistry lab, replete with beakers and pipettes, aprons, goggles, solutions, and so on. Because neither of us is a scientist, it brought back memories of our own high school and junior high years and the struggles we had to keep interest in the subject. But we pressed on, and sometime that afternoon we realized something: this was fun! Our daughter was really intent on the project and was doing a great job in measuring the solutions and going through the necessary steps of the experiment. Hours later, when we'd finished, we watched as she compiled the information and put together a really good poster for the science fair. She went into it confident that she'd done good work and happy for having spent time learning about the levels of vitamin C in different types of orange juice.

This was a learning experience for all of us, made possible not because of a creative idea but rather because of external circumstances that made it necessary. Self-knowledge is something we develop frequently as a result of the ideas we pursue and the talents we nourish, but it can also develop as a result of external demands. Someone at the school was responsible for proposing the science fair as an important learning experience for children. By submitting ourselves to that vision of the Good, we discovered something about ourselves.

Our role as parents is often analogous to that of the person who proposed a school science fair: we draw our children into learning experiences that they themselves might not have chosen but that grant them opportunities to develop self-knowledge and a vision of the Good. Ideally, one or more of these experiences lead to an "aha!" moment in their vocational discernment. We've both encountered young people who tell stories about wanting to be teachers, doctors, artists, lawyers, and so on because of the examples their parents set for them. Others talk about wanting marriages like those of their grandparents or parents or hoping to volunteer with the poor like a favorite aunt or even entering the priesthood like a beloved pastor.

> ## Vocation is about the persons we are, not just the work we do.

There is another implication of the lesson from the science fair, one that applies more to our role as adults and as parents. We too face life lessons we do not choose, and we too have opportunities to discover things about ourselves in those circumstances. Vocational discernment does not stop when we are adults; it continues throughout our lives. Too often people think of vocation as the work they do, and they consequently think primarily about training their children for types of work. Vocation, though, is about the persons we are, not just the work we do. Our work flows out of the kinds of people we are, but our vocation transcends the work we do at a given moment of our lives. In thinking about vocation, then, let us recall both for ourselves and for our children that discernment is first about how we choose to live in the world and only second about what kind of work we do.

CHAPTER TWENTY

DISCERNMENT FOR THE KINGDOM

Discernment is primarily oriented toward the question of what kinds of relationships we will form with others for the sake of building the Kingdom. All of us know this on some intuitive level. We care what others think about us. Sometimes we care too much and become compulsive in the ways that we present ourselves to the world, whether through the way we look or through the accomplishments we want to list on our résumés. But all of us want to be with people who bring out the best in us, whether at home or in the community or at work. And we want to help our kids learn the skills of engaging in good relationships while they are growing.

To put it another way, we are teaching our children about a vision of the world—the Kingdom—that is characterized by friendship rather

> We are teaching our children about a vision of the world—the Kingdom—that is characterized by friendship rather than competition.

than competition. This is a radical claim and deserves some explanation. Think for a moment about the distant hopes many have
for their children: going to college, getting a good job, marrying
a good person, and so on. And think about some of the ways our
social structures move them toward these goods: they have to get
certain grades in order to pass; they have to move from grade to
grade; they have to get into the college of their choice; and so on.
Notice, though, that it is possible at each level to approach the
good result with an attitude of either competition or friendship.
Are other students our competition for grades, or are they people
who can encourage us in learning? Are teammates people who are
competing for playtime, or are they people who help us improve
our game?

We've noticed that sometimes parents fall into patterns of competition that are unhealthy: think of the loud parent on the side-
lines whose rooting sounds more like complaining at the coach or
the alphaparent who ignores the advice of teachers and demands
his or her child be placed in all the honors classes. There can sometimes be a fine line between advocating for our children and over-
stepping our legitimate concern, particularly if our children have
special needs that require extraordinary efforts on our parts. The
great challenge, we are suggesting, is shepherding our children in
the direction of seeing others not as competitors but as friends.

One way we can help them learn to discern the Kingdom is by
carving out time for reflection on what's happened over the course
of a day or a week. In a fast-paced world, this can be enormously
difficult but also enormously rewarding. The children's version
of the Examen (see page 22) is one example. We've modified this
practice in different ways over the years in the hope of helping
them develop the habit of reflection, helping them focus more and
more on the ways they see God moving in their lives. Developing

the skill of living reflectively is one way we hope they will continue to grow spiritually.

Another way we help them practice discernment is the rather old-fashioned habit of learning the prayers of the Church. Prayers such as the Our Father, the Hail Mary, the Glory Be, and others give our children a language of faith they grow into. At different stages of their lives, as they learn the language of the Church—both in private prayer and in public liturgy—they come to new insights about the Bible stories that gave rise to the language and to the theology that helps them understand how God is at work in their lives. Far from empty, rote memorization, learning these prayers opens their vocabulary—and their understanding—as they grow older.

We see the practices of the Church—from the Eucharist to the various devotions and holidays and images and texts—as comprising a unique culture that can help our children thrive. Like the culture of

> The life of the Church can help children see the world as the beauty-filled place God loves enough to be part of, in the person of Jesus.

a country, Church culture provides a language, a community, a calendar of celebrations, heroes (the saints), a view of history, and so on. It can help shape a child's way of understanding the world. And at its best, it helps children see the world as the beauty-filled place God loves enough to be part of, in the person of Jesus. It points them toward discovering themselves as beloved children of God missioned to bring light to the suffering. It draws them to consider Christ as dwelling right in front of them, in the face of a friend or in the anguish of a child they don't even know. It helps them see their lives as saturated with meaning, inasmuch as God has chosen to call them into being out of great love and for the purpose of showing great love to others. And it invites them home again and again, in the midst of trial and pain, in the midst of joy and hope, to draw consolation from others who find the example of Jesus compelling as a blueprint for their own lives. We hope that the Eucharist, the shared encounter with the risen Christ, becomes for them the focal point of their lives because it helps them become conformed to the Body that gives itself for the life of that beloved world.

We want our children to be part of this culture, mindful that it sometimes fails to live up to what it seeks. Our Church has never been a perfect Church, but even when it has failed, it is still over-flowing with the grace of people who remember what it strives to be. To help our children discern their lives as the unfolding work of the Kingdom, we want them to encounter all sorts of ways that cultivate their imagination. From a theological standpoint, what we are encouraging is a sacramental worldview—that is, a sensibility that everything in the world is a potential place of transformative encounter with God. The Catholic understanding of sacraments rests upon the conviction that as author of all creation, God's fingerprints are everywhere, and the Holy Spirit lurks behind each face, each event, each effort for those who learn to look. By cultivating a sacramental imagination, we are hoping to help them have eyes to see.

What does this mean? Let us use a different image. Consider the parents who encourage their son or daughter to become a great athlete. Let's imagine a dad who wants his son to play football. He's a huge fan, having played in college, and he still watches college and pro football every weekend. He takes his young son to his alma mater for tailgates and games on Saturday; he takes the boy to pro games on Sunday. He signs his son up for Pop Warner football and coaches him up through middle school. He sends his son off to play for the local high school, where the boy is immersed in homecoming festivities, fans, cheerleaders, town parades, and so on. He graduates and is recruited to play at the college level. As an athlete on campus, he's held in awe by other students. He is living life to the full. It is very likely that such a young man will come to see the world often through the lens of competition: those who have talent succeed; those who lack talent are cut from the team. It is further likely that this young man will see much of the world through his football experiences. He will have traveled to other schools to play games. He will have learned how to interact with adults through his interactions with coaches and teachers. He will have developed a self-image that owes a great deal to the way these same adults view his ability to play football. He will interact with his peers in ways shaped by how they view him as a player; perhaps his relationships with women will be similarly shaped.

Parents immerse their children in different kinds of culture as they grow up; this example of playing football is but one of many. There are cultures related to various professions, political stances, artistic or academic interests, ethnic groups, and so on. We are proposing the culture of the Church as a kind of "superculture" in the etymological sense: *super* (above or beyond) a given *cultura* (growing)—that is, a way of growing together those who are embedded in smaller communities of growth. Every culture has its limits, and not every child will be interested in the same things his or her parents train him or her to embrace. The superculture of the Church aims to draw people to use their various talents toward the building of the Kingdom, to become Christ's Body in the world.

And so we hope our children will learn to navigate this superculture of the Church, to learn its language and its various groups and its hopes for a just and beautiful world. We want to give them many tools in their spiritual toolkit: prayers in different languages, practices from different cultures, rituals for various occasions, artistic representations of biblical stories and great saints, stories etched in stained glass and in novels and in architecture around the world. Most importantly, we want them to understand what is probably the most countercultural position of the Church in the modern and postmodern world: that their spiritual lives are never only a private matter. No. We want them to understand that their faith impels them to look at the world the way Christ did and to reach out to others to heal the broken world in ways that only a gathered community can.

GOING TO CHURCH

Consider the Church as the place where you "culture" your children in habits of love. Here are our top ten reasons (in no particular order) for going to church and for wanting our children to grow in this community.

1. Encountering a community that hopes to be Christ in the world: concrete men, women, and children who want their lives to show what it means that God so loved the world as to send his only Son.

2. Celebrating the sacraments, the rituals by which we and our children mark significant moments in our lives as they have been touched and shaped by encounter with Jesus.

3. Developing a sense of history, of connection to the people and texts that have exemplified what it means to live in faith that God is active in people's lives.

4. Learning about the saints, the men and women whose lives have overflowed with love for the world and who teach us new ways of thinking about love.

5. Being formed in a language of love rather than a language of competition or money or selfishness.

6. Meeting other families at every life stage and every social and economic background.

7. Being challenged to think more generously, more expansively, more actively about how we can be gifts to others.
8. Developing a global vision by connecting with others around the entire world who similarly pray using the same texts, words, and beliefs.
9. Having a sense of home in other parts of the country and other parts of the world. Anywhere there is a church, there are members of the family.
10. Working toward a more just world by gathering together with others to build a culture of love rooted in Jesus' teachings.

CONCLUSION

BEYOND THE RULES

In a word, family spirituality is about hope. It is about living with people of different ages, all of whom have hopes and desires for their lives. It is about carving out a shared life around things like meals and work and school and activities. It is about making choices big and small on a daily basis. We have tried to suggest a shared spirituality that will enhance family life and orient it toward a shared desire to bring forth the Kingdom.

The rules we explored in part one of this book are rooted in centuries of Christian wisdom. Ultimately, they point to a simple truth: life with God is better than life without God, and life with others is a privileged way of encountering God in love. To use Saint Augustine's pithy summary, "love, and do what you will."

There is a helpful image that comes from the 1996 film *Shine* about the Australian pianist David Helfgott. The image comes from Helfgott's musical education, but it can be applied more generally to our hopes as parents. At one point in the film, we see Helfgott with his teacher, Parkes. Helfgott starts bashing away at the piano, but Parkes stops him to remind him to pay attention to the notes on the page. "The notes first," he says. "Your interpretation comes on top of them." Parkes wants Helfgott, at least for a time, to pay primary attention not to the kind of raw emotion that Helfgott feels inside himself but rather to the rules that any student must learn before he or she can begin to develop as an artist. Parkes does not negate Helfgott's emotions; he instructs Helfgott that to interpret and share his emotions properly, he must lay the proper groundwork.

The vocation to parenthood is similar to the role that Parkes plays in Helfgott's life. Children (as well as adults) are filled with every sort of emotion, and left unchecked, those emotions can lead to conflict. The wrong response to a child's emotional life is to believe emotion is wrong or that children should focus solely on obedience. Instead, we want to teach them to pay attention to their emotions and what those feelings suggest to them about the kinds of people God has created them to be. The rules are not fundamentally about trying to get everyone to do the same things and keeping people from fighting with one another. Rather, they are about helping people young and old to live life to the full as God intended. To do this, the rules are like "the notes first," that is, they are about learning good habits that children (and adults) will understand more and more as they grow older. Ultimately, the rules, like the notes, are in service to a beauty that is grander than the sum of its parts. True love, like true art, is more than imitation: It is creative. It is fresh. It is new. Cultivating a family spirituality is ultimately about helping our children listen to a God who is ever "doing a new thing" (cf. Is 43:19)—finding new ways to invite people to be love in the world in cooperation with God.

APPENDIX

SPIRITUAL PRACTICES FOR PARENTS AND FAMILIES

FOR PARENTS

1. Pray the rules. Read them slowly and use them to speak directly to God.

    You have created our family for a purpose: to praise and serve you through the way we love one another as a family. Help us not lose sight of that purpose. Help us find you even in financial trouble, stress at work or school, sickness, or even death. Help us find joy in our daily lives together, and help us build your Kingdom of justice and love and mercy and beauty together. Help us learn to celebrate the coming of your Kingdom right at home. And please help us come to desire you and all the things that bring about your Kingdom; assist us in letting go of the small desires that hold us back from becoming free.

2. Plan a day away from the kids and spend time reflecting in a journal. If there are two of you, spend part of the day alone and the other part of the day talking through what you've written. Consider some or all of these questions to get you started:

   a. Do I believe God has made me for a purpose?

   b. When in my life have I felt most sure of God?

   c. When in my life have I felt least sure of God?

   d. What have been my experiences of prayer?

3. Mark out a time each day for two weeks to reinvigorate your prayer life; treat it like you would a new workout or diet that requires effort to establish good habits. Talk with others in your family about why this effort is important and ask for their support (like not bothering you during that time).

4. Consider new ways of praying.

   a. Learn a traditional devotion like the Rosary.

   b. Use your imagination to picture yourself in a biblical story. Different seasons offer good examples, such as the stories around Jesus' birth during the Christmas season (Mt 1:18–2:23 and Lk 1:5–2:40) or the stories of Jesus' death and resurrection during the Lenten and Easter seasons.

5. Read the Sunday gospels during the week and come to greater awareness of the liturgical year. You can find the readings on the US Bishops' website at http://www.usccb.org/bible/readings.

6. Read books, magazines, or blogs about how to live your faith. Build your own strong foundation, so you can share it more easily with your children. Pay attention to the rhythms of the liturgical year by reading the various texts used in daily Mass.

7. Read entire books of the Bible in one sitting or two (many are short enough to get through fairly quickly). Note: it's not a particularly good idea to read the Bible cover to cover, as the collection is not in chronological or thematic order. Get a good book introducing the Old and New Testaments or a good study Bible like the *Catholic Study Bible* and follow its recommendation for reading.

8. Read through Mark's gospel (the oldest), then later go back and read each of the other gospels to see comparisons and contrasts. Get to know how each evangelist portrays Jesus and ask what each was trying to teach his followers.

9. Try praying the Divine Office (also known as the Liturgy of the Hours), an ancient monastic form of prayer that relies heavily on the Psalms. You can get apps for your phone (look up "breviary," which is a Latin name referring to the little book that clerics use to recite it daily). You can also go to www.universalis.com.

10. Try other forms of scriptural prayer like www.sacredspace.ie (which offers a guided mediation on a scriptural text online) and www.pray-as-you-go.org (which offers a podcast with a daily reading).

11. Practice praying the Examen on a regular basis (see page 20), developing your own awareness of God's presence in daily life.

12. Use a journal to begin a list of people and things you are thankful for on a daily basis.

13. Make a local pilgrimage to a shrine or a cathedral and learn about the art and architecture.

14. Preface all your family's important decisions with prayer and ask for God's blessing on the decision. Try on the different options and imagine yourself living with each of them; pay attention to what feelings the decision elicits.

FOR FAMILIES

1. To the extent possible with your children, carve out quiet time when there are no screens being used (TV, computer, phone, etc.). Allow for quiet play or conversation regularly so that the family's attention is shared around one thing, not fragmented into many things.

2. Make a habit of praying together before meals. Use a simple prayer that the youngest of your children can understand, even if it's as simple as "Thanks, God, for this food."

3. Introduce God into ordinary conversation. For example, introduce God into conversations about things you're thankful for or hopeful about. Tell your children about what you ask God for and why you turn to God when you are in pain.

4. Use a photo album to show your children the members of your family of origin and talk about what kind of people they are (or were). Help young children name the kind of people they want to be.

5. Ask small children what they dream about being when they grow up. Help them talk about their goals in life.

6. At bedtime, ask your children to talk about their day. What made them happy? What made them sad? What do they look forward to tomorrow?

7. Show children how you go out of your way to build the Kingdom by taking them to serve a meal to an elderly neighbor, to help at a shelter, or to do work at the church.

8. If you don't do it already, start going to church regularly. Meet people there and learn why they go. Treat going to church like going to the gym: as a way of keeping you and your family practiced in the spiritual life. Be open to the Church's witness about this regular encounter with the living Jesus in the Eucharist, which fuels our growth in faith, hope, and love. Let yourself be challenged by Saint Paul's exhortation to "pray without ceasing."

9. Find age-appropriate ways to practice habits of reflection in daily life: looking back at the day at bedtime, sharing stories of the day over a meal, saying a short reflective prayer before Mass.

10. Take your children to a historic church and explain the art they see.

11. Get a children's Bible and read the stories of Jesus' birth at Christmas with your children.

12. Read the stories of Jesus' passion and death during Holy Week.

13. Read the stories of Easter during Easter week.

14. Teach your children the prayer of imagination: seeing themselves in Bible stories and talking with Jesus about what they experience.

15. Find good printed resources to help your children learn the rhythms of the Church year.

NOTES

1. The text is usually rendered "repent, for the kingdom of heaven is at hand." The Greek verb is *metanoiete*, which literally means "change your minds." As we'll suggest, a life rooted in transformative love is an opportunity to change our way of looking at the world.

2. For more on the theme of friendship with God, see the series by William Barry, S.J.: *A Friendship Like No Other: Experiencing God's Amazing Embrace* (Chicago: Loyola Press, 2008); *Changed Heart, Changed World: The Transforming Freedom of Friendship with God* (Chicago: Loyola Press, 2011); and *Praying the Truth: Deepening Your Friendship with God through Honest Prayer* (Chicago: Loyola Press, 2012).

3. The phrase comes from the Carmelite William McNamara, describing contemplation, but it also derives from the essay of the same title by Walter Burghardt, S.J., reprinted in George Traub, S.J., ed., *An Ignatian Spirituality Reader* (Chicago: Loyola Press, 2008), 89–98.

4. "Hope in God—Creator," written on March 1, 1855. *Meditations and Devotions of the Late Cardinal Newman* (New York: Longman, Green, and Company, 1911), 301.

5. Thomas Merton, *Thoughts in Solitude* (New York: Farrar, Straus and Giroux, 1999), 79.

6. The Rosenows operate The Shepherd's Crook Ministries (http://theshepherdscrook.org/about/rosenows/), which helps families adopt special-needs children around the world. They recently wrote a book detailing their family's story.

7. Greg Boyle, S.J., *Tattoos on the Heart* (New York: Simon and Schuster, 2010), 178.

8. For a better understanding of the Old Testament, we recommend using a good study Bible, such as *The Catholic Study Bible* (Oxford University Press) or the *Saint Mary's Press College Study Bible*. Lawrence Boadt's *Reading the Old Testament* (revised and updated by Richard Clifford and Daniel Harrington; Mahwah, NJ: Paulist Press, 2012) is a good supplementary text.

9. Mark's use of the Greek verb *egeirein* makes it clear he wants to connote that Jesus raised her from the dead rather than just awakening her from a sleep.

10. Examples include picking grain and healing on Sabbath days: Matthew 12:1–8 and Mark 3:1–6.

TIM MULDOON is a professor and author/editor of several books. He served as chair of the Department of Religious Studies, Philosophy, and Theology at Mount Aloysius College for a number of years before being named the inaugural director of the Church in the 21st Century Center at Boston College. He currently serves in the Division of University Mission and Ministry at Boston College, and teaches in the university's College of Arts and Sciences.

SUE MULDOON is a therapist and religious educator who has worked in clinical, collegiate, and parish settings. Her clinical work has focused on young adults and children. She worked for many years in college counseling at Saint Vincent College and Saint Francis University, and she has worked as a Director of Religious Education for Good Shepherd Parish in Wayland, Massachusetts. She and Tim are the parents of three children.

Founded in 1865, Ave Maria Press,
a ministry of the Congregation of
Holy Cross, is a Catholic publishing
company that serves the spiritual and
formative needs of the Church and its
schools, institutions, and ministers;
Christian individuals and families; and
others seeking spiritual nourishment.

For a complete listing of titles from

Ave Maria Press

Sorin Books

Forest of Peace

Christian Classics

visit www.avemariapress.com

ave maria press® / Notre Dame, IN 46556
A Ministry of the United States Province of Holy Cross